# THE BEST OF THE WEST

## GAA Greats of Connacht

*But – hark! – some voice like thunder spake*
*The West's awake, the West's awake.*

*To the memory of*
*Joan and Michael Campbell*

# THE BEST OF THE WEST

## GAA Greats of Connacht

# John Scally

The Collins Press

Published in 2008 by
The Collins Press
West Link Park
Doughcloyne
Wilton
Cork

British Library Cataloguing in Publication Data

Scally, John
    The best of the west : GAA greats of Connacht
    1. Gaelic Athletic Association - History - 20th century
    2. Gaelic games - Ireland - Connacht - History 3. Gaelic
    football players - Ireland - Connacht - Interviews
    I. Title
    796'.094171

ISBN-13: 9781905172825

Design and typesetting by edit+

Printed in Malta by Gutenberg Press Ltd

**Mixed Sources**
Product group from well-managed
forests, and other controlled sources
www.fsc.org  Cert no. TT-CoC-002424
© 1996 Forest Stewardship Council
FSC

The paper used for this book is FSC-certified and
totally chlorine-free. FSC (the Forest Stewardship
Council) is an international network to promote
responsible management of the world's forests.

# Contents

# Acknowledgements

This book would not have been possible without the wonderful generousity of my interviewees. I am grateful for their time, co-operation, humour, insights, dream teams and photos. Special thanks go to Johnny Hughes for dedication above and beyond the call of duty.

Family members of those players who have passed on have also been very helpful, notably Frances Morley, Mary Colette Gallagher, Ann Colleran and Joanne McDonagh. John Murray was more generous than Santa Claus in his eagerness to help. Seamus Heaney speaks of 'the economy of kindness'. In that economy John Purcell is a market-leader and I am particularly grateful to him for his help. Enda Kenny, as passionate and as knowledgeable a Mayo fan as I ever met, was very helpful to me as were his brothers Henry and John. Dermot Flanagan was also extremely helpful.

Every GAA manager brings joy to the fans of a county team, some when they arrive, more often when they leave! John O'Mahony has always been in the former category. I am very honoured that John agreed to write the foreword of this book particularly in the light of his involvement with teams in Mayo, Galway, Leitrim, Roscommon and indeed the Connacht team. However, I am particularly honoured by his friendship down the years.

I am forever indebted to Tony Conboy for kindly putting his wonderful collection of photos at my disposal. Dave O'Connell of the *Connacht Tribune* was characteristically good-humoured when his help was sought with photos. His colleague Joe O'Shaughnessy was also very helpful. Henry Wills of the *Western People* was more than generous in donating photos. Noel Fallon of the *Roscommon Champion* was typically gracious and accommodating with photos as was the paper's ace photographer Gerard O'Loughlin. *The Westmeath-Offaly Independent* were also helpful with photos as was Leo Gray of *The Sligo Champion*.

Thanks to Damien Eagers, Nicola Dihrberg, Cormac Murphy, Mary O'Neill, Preta Prendergast and Teresa Scally for their help with photos. I am grateful to the ever helpful Seamus Scally and Eamon Campion for their practical assistance and to Micheál Ó Muircheartaigh and Jimmy Magee who shared their vast reservoir of GAA knowledge with me and to the last remaining survivor of Mayo's All-Ireland winning triumph in 1936, Tom McNicholas for putting his memories at my disposal.

I am grateful to Katy Dobey, a star in the making, for sending me her poem 'When we went walking together'. As I was writing this book, Ollie Campbell was in my thoughts a lot. I salute his positive attitude.

I am also grateful to Joao Soares of Shannonside-Northern Sound for his help in recent times. Thanks to Con Collins, Gillian Hennessy and The Collins Press for their support.

*Below:* You got to have faith: John O'Mahony puts on a brave face after Mayo lose the 1989 All-Ireland final to Cork. *Photo:* Western People/*Henry Wills*

# Foreword

Since its foundation, the GAA has produced many heroes. Connacht has contributed numerous individuals to this honour list and though sometimes overshadowed by the other provinces, the heroes recognised in this book are undoubtedly of a calibre equal to the greatest sportspeople countrywide from the GAA itself and many other sports.

Of the individuals included in this book, I grew up in great admiration of some of the stars of the past, the skills and exploits of the 'terrible twins' Seán Purcell and Frank Stockwell, the grace and style of Paddy Prendergast, Leitrim's Packy McGarty, Sligo's Micheál Kearins, the physical presence and leadership of Dermot Earley, and the 'never say die' approach of Declan Darcy and Mickey Quinn and, of course, Galway's many hurling legends. Throughout my own involvement with the GAA, I have also either played with or managed stars of the more recent past and present such as Kevin Walsh, Martin Carney and Eamonn O'Hara.

Indeed, having spent my life in GAA playing and working with players at club, county and provincial levels in Connacht, I have been privileged to work with players from all five counties of Connacht in one respect or another, some of whom have been recognised in these pages. This experience has taught me that while there will always be great battles among these players within the province, they are equally united in their common desire to see the spoils of victory return across the Shannon.

I believe that the players honoured by this book epitomise the very best of Gaelic games and sport in this country. They have contributed richly to the heritage of the GAA in Connacht and Ireland and indeed some, notably Alan Kerins and John Tiernan, have distinguished themselves both on the field as outstanding players and further by providing leadership and vision in the wider community. I am delighted to see the talents and successes of all those recognised in this book.

I have no doubt that this book will inspire others to emulate the achievements of the individuals it recognises and as such, it is a significant contribution not only to the history but also to the practice of Gaelic games in Connacht.

John O'Mahony, September 2008

# Introduction

Ultimately Gaelic games are a spiritual experience: on a plane far higher than mere entertainment. Their liturgy is the merging of a collective spirit, the unification of minds that call every man, woman and child of a county unit at home and abroad to the altar of worship. They bring life to people and make it good to be alive. Their rituals are sacraments of the body and soul of a people – celebrations of a past that is noble, a present that is proud and a future that will be magical. Their prayers mystically invoke love of the traditions, culture and way of life associated with the faithful's home and place of origin, the club or county that nurtures a sense of belonging and identity. Their cathedrals reveal what was, is and is to come by telling us who we are and where we come from.

This book pays homage to great games, great heroes and great people. We age but memories of their magic moments and beguiling brilliance do not. The annals of the GAA have a special place for the famous players who, by their genius on the field over a period of years, have claimed a permanent place in the memory of all who love the game. It is a debt that the GAA can never repay. Every county has furnished its stars. This book celebrates some of the stars of the Connacht counties.

The most difficult part of writing this book was to decide which players to feature. I was spoilt for choice and acutely conscious that no matter what route I took I was not going to please everybody. History has forged a peculiarly close bond between these five counties. No other province has had to live with the noose around its neck of 'To hell or to Connacht'. Nonetheless the solidarity off the field is matched only by the intense rivalry between the counties on it. No two Connacht fans would produce an identical top forty players.

To come close to cataloguing all the great players who have lined out for the Connacht counties I would need ten books not one. I am not claiming that the players celebrated in this book are the greatest players. Several of them certainly are but some pundits and fans may query some of my selection choices. In that respect, as this volume clearly demonstrates, I follow the tradition of the county selectors! This is not the last word on this topic, just the first word.

I could have filled the book with profiles of the Roscommon team of

1943 and 1944, the Mayo team from 1950 and 1951 and the Galway team of 1964–66 alone. However, the task I set myself in this book is twofold: to pay homage to the legends of Connacht football and hurling; and to write an entertaining book. In doing so I may have stretched the definition of 'best of the west' in the eyes of some to get as much diversity and colour in the profiles as possible. Eugene McGee once incurred the wrath of Galway fans when he spoke of the 'fancy Dans' on John O'Mahony's side. While the book features many of the acknowledged giants of the game I was also keen to include some players I had often witnessed at first hand whose lack of celebrity did not diminish their profound impact on a pitch and whose commitment to the cause was no less when their side was ten points down in a League match on a windswept, soggy pitch in January as in Croke Park on a glorious summer's day.

I have had this project in my mind for years and publish for the first time interviews with some of the best of the west who have passed on to their eternal reward such as Jimmy Murray, Seán Purcell and Enda Colleran. The book is based largely on interviews so it is heavily biased towards the living and therefore I am regretfully not featuring players who died before I could interview them such as Mayo's Tom Langan, arguably the finest full-forward of all time.

I, of course, had to include some of 'the giants of the ash' from Galway down the years. Again, I was spoilt for choice and restricted myself to a magnificent seven hurling legends.

This book celebrates more than just genius on the playing fields. In a speech he made shortly before his death in 1968, Robert Kennedy said: 'Each of us can work to change a small portion of events, and in the total of all those acts will be written the history of this generation. It is from the numberless diverse acts of courage and belief that human history is shaped. Each time a man stands up for an ideal, or acts to improve the lot of others, or strikes out against injustice, he sends a tiny ripple of hope, and crossing each other from a million different centres of energy and daring, those ripples build a current which can sweep down the mightiest walls of oppression and resistance.'

The book concludes with the stories of two remarkable players who, in their commitment to the downtrodden of the developing world, personify the best of the west. Fittingly, though, it begins with the greatest player of them all.

John Scally, September 2008

# The Flair Factor

From JOHN D. HICKEY.
NEW YORK. MONDAY.


While I will even give an attentive ear to those
who contend that Christy Rink is the best hurler
of all time - my own choice has ever been Mick
Mackey - I have in the last ten days become utterly
intolerant of those who argue that there ever has
been a better footballer than Galway's Sean Purcell.

I have always held the Tuam player in very high
esteem, but having seen the sheer football sorcery
of the man last Sunday week at the Polo Grounds and
yesterday at Gaelic Park where Galway drew 2-7 to
2-7 with New York I am convinced he is the best of
all time.

What a football brain the man has, how contemptuous
he is of his own personal safety when his side is in
peril and how light he makes of real injury when the
honour of Galway is at stake.

Some may vehemently argue that John Joe Sheehy had
more football sense, that Paddy Bawn Brosnan was more
daring and that "Gunner" Brady was more durable, but
with all due respect to those stars of other days I
doubt if a combination of all three would equal the
Purcell we have seen here.

We all know that he has often been a football host at
home, but not even his best in Ireland approaches the
magnificence of his displays here.

It was as if he came out obsessed with the idea of showing greybeard exiles that talk that the men of to-day
were geese compared to swans of other football eras was
all moonshine and how he has succeeded in exploding the
myth.

Almost as striking as the football powers of the man is
his modesty. When I congratulated him after those two
displays that I will ever cherish in the storehouse of
my memories he was genuinely embarrassed.


....oOo....

2

# The Master

## Seán Purcell

When I asked Jimmy Magee who was the greatest Gaelic footballer he had ever seen, the answer came with a prologue:

'I love picking dream teams. Pat Spillane would have to be on a dream team, as would Mike Sheehy. The big problem with such a team would be to select which three Kerry players at midfield: Paddy Kennedy, Jack O'Shea and Mick O'Connell. I'll always remember playing a match with the Jimmy Magee All-Stars when my son, who was a handy player, went up for a ball only for Mick O'Connell to soar like an eagle and take it off him. My son said to me afterwards, "That man is in his fifties. What must he have been like in his prime?"

'Having said all of that about the Kerry lads, the first man I would have on a team of all-time greats would be Galway's Seán Purcell.'

Micheál Ó Muircheartaigh had this to say about the greatest player of all time: 'I will say that the best display I ever saw was by Galway's Seán Purcell. Most people remember him as a great Galway forward and for his association with Frankie Stockwell. Mayo had the best full-forward of the time, some would say of all time, Tom Langan, and Galway pulled off a shock move by bringing Seán back to mark him, and he gave the finest performance I ever saw. I saw him later that year in the All-Ireland semi-final against Kerry and he was outstanding. Kerry were winning well and late in the game Galway moved him to midfield and he almost swung it for them. He had such skill and style that you could play him anywhere.'

After seeing Purcell play, the noted GAA writer John D. Hickey was moved to write a letter which survives in its original form.

My only meeting with Seán Purcell is a memory that will stay with me forever.

*Preceding page:* Galway and Cork go man to man in the 1956 All-Ireland final (from left): Sean Keeley takes on Johnny Creedon while Billy O'Neill restrains Neily Duggan and Niall Fitzgerald looks on. Note: Sean Purcell is playing but out of shot.
*Left:* The letter from John D. Hickey.

He transmitted vitality and enthusiasm like electricity. He considers himself to be a lucky man.

'I was born in Tuam, one of the great heartlands of Gaelic football. We have more than the Saw Doctors you know! I went to school in what is one of Ireland's finest football nurseries in St Jarlath's College. One of the highlights of my life was when winning an All-Ireland colleges title with them in 1946.'

In his early days in the maroon of Galway he was in the right place at the wrong time.

'I came on the inter-county scene in the late 1940s. Mayo had a wonderful team and overshadowed us for years. I will never forget one day they beat us very badly in Tuam. I happened to be in Galway that night and I met a great old friend of mine, Mayo's greatest ever forward Tom Langan. Tom was a very quiet man who didn't have much to say. But he had a few pints that night and he came over to me and he said: "Don't let that worry you. I played in six Connacht finals before I won one." I think that gave me heart. Before we played Mayo in the Connacht Championship in '54 we decided we had to give it everything, that we had a chance. We beat them against all the odds and after that then we took off. From there on, things fell into position easily enough.

'I was picked at full-back for that Mayo match. We led by 2-3 to 0-1 at half-time but Mayo came at us with all guns blazing and we held out for a one point win. I enjoyed playing there but I think the powers that be felt that I might be better deployed further up the field and I switched to attack. I think most people think I only ever played at centre-forward! The great advantage of that position was that it allowed me to control what the media today rejoice in calling "the attacking channels".'

The 1956 All-Ireland final was the apex of the team's achievement when they beat Cork by 2-13 to 3-7.

'We had a great lead at half-time and Cork came back to us in a big way. They really put it up to us and they got back within a point or so. We were lucky enough to get back one or two points at the end.

'We got a wonderful reception at home. I remember that quite well, coming from Dublin into Tuam. By present day standards the crowd was not huge but it was a great night. The match was broadcast around the town that day and there would have been a great spirit of victory around

*Left:* The three wise men: Seán Purcell is flanked by two of the legends of Connacht football – Tull Dunne (on the right) and Brendan Nestor after the 1956 All-Ireland final against Cork.

the place. When we arrived in Tuam I think the crowd met us and we were carried shoulder-high or on the lorry down to the town.'

Another national honour came the following year when Galway beat Kerry by 1-8 to 0-7 in the League final. Kerry, captained by Mick O'Connell, got their revenge in the All-Ireland final in 1959 when they beat the Westerners by 3-7 to 1-4.

'I made a stupid mistake early on. I was playing full-forward. My opponent Niall Sheehy was a big strong man and the ball was going wide. I could have left it go but I saw Niall coming towards me. I said I'd get my retaliation in first and I did. I hit him an almighty crack with my forearm across the head and he got in under me and he put me up in the air. I really thought I had killed him but when I looked up all he did was shake his head a few times and trot away. It was a bad start, a foolish mistake and after that we were well beaten. We didn't really make much of a show. The lads did their best all right but we just weren't good enough that day.'

Purcell has amassed an impressive roll-call of honours.

'Of course winning the All-Ireland was the highlight but winning Connacht titles in 1954, '56, '57, '58, '59 and '60 were great moments, as was winning the League title. People today have no appreciation of how massive the Railway Cups were back in the 1950s. It would be unfair to say it was on a par with winning the All-Ireland but it wasn't far behind. The crowds were massive and the atmosphere was magical. The Railway Cups I won with Connacht in 1951, '57 and '58 were all real highlights. Of course, because the club is so important in the GAA, winning ten county Championships with Tuam Stars was wonderful. After I retired I had two lovely honours when I was chosen at centre-forward for the Football Team of the Century and later I was selected in the Football Team of the Millennium in 1999.'

There is a school of thought, though, which suggests that the greatest honour to Purcell was the massive attendance at his funeral in 2005. He died, following a brief illness, at the age of seventy-five.

Purcell's final Championship game in a Galway shirt witnessed an incident which has become part of GAA folklore. In the 1962 Connacht final Roscommon trailed Galway by five points with less than ten minutes to go and looked like a beaten side. A Galway forward took a shot and put his team six points up. As the ball was cutting like a bullet over the crossbar, the Roscommon goalie, the late Aidan Brady, a big man, jumped up and hung on the crossbar and it broke.

*Right:* Nothing compares to you: The late, very great Seán Purcell in 1954.

'There was a lengthy delay until a new crossbar was found. The delay disrupted our rhythm and allowed Roscommon to snatch victory from the jaws of defeat thanks to a vintage display from Gerry O'Malley. I remember talking to Gerry while we were waiting for them to fix the crossbar. He said to me: "It's probably gone from us. We can't turn it around now." Then he went to midfield and they got two goals to tie things up. When they equalised Gerry ran over to the Roscommon fans who were on the sideline and asked them how much time was left. They said that time was up. He won the ball and put Des Feeley through for the winning point.'

Seán Purcell's name, good nature and face lives on in his son John, who played Championship football for Galway in 1985 and who continues to maintain the family friendship with Purcell's teammate Frank Stockwell. With a twinkle in his eye, John recalls his father's mischievous nature:

'Daddy had a great capacity to become friends with a large section of people. Seán Óg Ó hAlpín was just one of the people who visited him in hospital. He became very friendly with the Dublin team of the 1970s through his role in managing the All-Stars, especially with Tony Hanahoe. They have a charity function every year and present Hall of Fame style awards. The night before Dad died they were presenting Martin O'Neill and himself with an award and I was accepting it on his behalf. I asked him had he any message for them. He replied: "Tell them before I got to know them I thought they were a crowd of f**kers but once I got to know them I didn't think they were too bad!" I said a softer version of that on the night!

'One time he was collecting an award himself up north and the MC was going on and on about how great a player Daddy had been. Daddy grabbed the microphone off him in midflow and said: "Don't think I'm that famous. I ran for election once. Both John Donnellan and I were running for Fine Gael for the one seat in 1965. I barely got my deposit back and was lucky to get even that and John was easily elected. As I was leaving the count centre crestfallen a woman called me over and said: "Don't worry Seánin, there'll be another day. Isn't it a pity you didn't play a bit of football!"

I asked Seán to select the greatest team of players he had seen since he retired from the game. It was:

1. Johnny Geraghty
(Galway)

2. Enda Colleran
(Galway)

3. Noel Tierney
(Galway)

4. Tom O'Hare
(Down)

5. John Donnellan
(Galway)

6. Kevin Moran
(Dublin)

7. Martin Newell
(Galway)

8. Brian Mullins
(Dublin)

9. Jack O'Shea
(Kerry)

10. Dermot Earley
(Roscommon)

11. Micheál Kearins
(Sligo)

12. Pat Spillane
(Kerry)

13. Packy McGarty
(Leitrim)

14. Seán O'Neill
(Down)

15. Mike Sheehy
(Kerry)

# The Man With The Magic Hands

## Henry Kenny

Henry Kenny was a man ahead of time. Long before sports psychology became fashionable he innately understood its power. He was the star player on Mayo's first All-Ireland winning team in 1936 and when Kerry next faced the Westerners their great midfielder Johnny Walsh was given a very simple instruction by the Kerry management: 'Flatten Henry Kenny.' In line with instructions, Walsh sent Kenny sprawling. As he looked up from the ground at his opponent's feet, the Mayo star calmly said: 'Johnny, what did you do that for?' In an era when players met fire with fire Walsh was so taken aback by Kenny's passivity that he was unable to concentrate on the match and very uncharacteristically barely touched the ball for the rest of the game. Apart from his All-Ireland medal Kenny won seven National League medals, three Railway Cups and six Connacht Championships.

From his office in Dáil Eireann Fine Gael leader Enda Kenny is understandably proud of his father's achievements.

'In 1935 Kerry had refused to play in the Championship as a gesture of solidarity with interned prisoners in the Curragh. In 1936 they were back but Mayo ended their interest in Championship in the All-Ireland semi-final and Dad was seen as the star, especially as he was in the glamour position of midfield. In today's terms he was a superstar. It was only when I got involved in politics that I came to realise just how revered he was by older people in particular. A mythology developed in the county about the '36 team, not least because they went fifty-three games without defeat. People thought they could jump over telegraph poles.

'My father went to teacher training college in De La Salle Waterford. One of his fellow students was Seán Brosnan, who became a Fianna Fáil T.D. for Cork. Times were very tough and the food was so scarce there that my father said you needed to have the plates nailed to the tables! After he qualified he went to teach in Connemara and cycled sixteen miles to train for the club team and sixty miles to Castlebar to play for Mayo. One of his teammates was Paddy Moclair who was the first Bank official to play county football and he cycled from Clare. I've seen telegrams from the time

CUMANN LUIT-CLEAS GAEDEAL. CONNDAE MUIGEO.

Claremorris,
3/ 7/ 37.

To each member of the Team.

A Chara,

        After a triumphant tour in the U.S.A. Mayo enter the 1937 Championships with a proud record. To maintain the high place, so richly deserved, it is important that each member of the Team be fighting fit. Many consider that a Team loses form by reason of a tour in the U.S.A. so it is up to you to prove that such is not the case.

        For the match against Galway on July 18th. each member is expected to train strenuously from now until Tuesday July 13th. From past experience you know the nature of the training to undergo. It is not possible to bring the members of the team together, but the Co. Board expects each member to do his part. Will you do your part.

Do A Chara,
S. Omaille.

*Above:* An unusual self-help manual!

from the Mayo County Board and they were told: "Train yourself. You've been selected to play".

    'Football training included a standing jump practice. A football was tied on a piece of string and raised on a pulley. The higher you jumped, the higher the pulley was raised. Another form of training included large road mileage in heavy boots.

    'In 1936 the Mayo team were invited down to play Kerry in the opening match in Fitzgerald Stadium. There were seven or eight of them in the car on the way home. They left for Mayo on the Sunday night and whether it was the signs or the driver that was at fault they found themselves in Carlow the next morning. They were all starving and went to a café for breakfast only to discover that nobody had any money to pay for it. Moclair

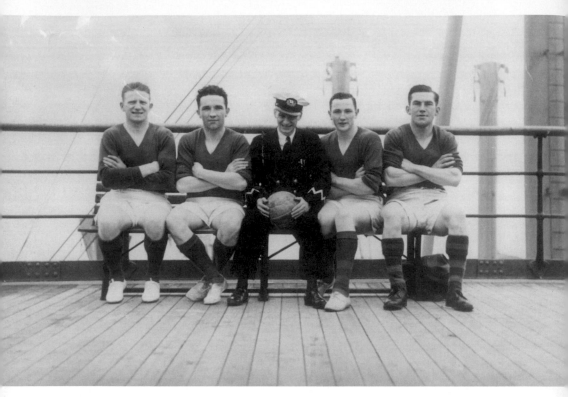

*Above:* Ship Ahoy (from left): Patsy Flannelly, Paddy Moclair, the captain of the ship, Henry Kenny and Purty Kelly as the Mayo team sailed to America in 1937.

told the rest of them that he would cause a diversion and the rest of them were to make a run for it!

'Another time they were driving home from a match and were dropping my father off in Connemara very late in the night when the car plunged into a stream. There must have been a few drinks taken because nobody was too worried and they all fell asleep in the car. When they woke up there were forty or fifty people with shovels round the car. They thought that all the players were dead!

'My father was particularly famous for his fielding of the ball. He grew up on the same street with Patsy Flannelly, another of the stars of the '36 team. They had no football as kids so they went to the butcher's shop and got pigs' bladders from him to use instead of footballs. Dad always said: "If you could catch those you could catch anything."

'The other thing he was noted for was his ability, after he caught the ball in the air, to turn before his feet touched the ground. When my brothers and I started playing his advice to us was always: "Be moving before the ball

*Above:* Casino Royale: The 1936 All-Ireland winning Mayo team visit a casino on their victory tour to America. Fourth from the left is the last surviving member of the team, Tom McNicholas who stands beside Henry Kenny (fifth from left).

comes." He found a big change in the way the game was played, especially when they started wearing lighter boots like the soccer players. When he saw a pair of them he said: "These boots are like slippers." He didn't have much time for the solo runs and that's why he called it "the tippy toe". He said he would "beat the solo runner with his cap".

'Dad had great admiration for athletes. That's probably why the player he admired most was Kildare's Larry Stanley.'

Henry Kenny's footballing genes were to some extent passed on to his sons.

'My brother Kieran played at midfield for Mayo. His finest hour personally was the 1979 Connacht final when he gave the great Dermot Earley a bit of a roasting. In saying that I might be a little biased! Injury though meant that he retired prematurely. I was on the fringes of the Mayo team myself when I was first elected to the Dáil in 1975. I always say I was called to a bigger pitch for a bigger battle.'

Enda Kenny is himself part of a mixed marriage. He married the daughter of a Kerry footballer.

'Our three children are unusual in that both of their grandfathers have won senior All-Ireland medals. Their maternal grandfather, Seán Kelly, won an All-Ireland with Kerry in 1953.'

In 1954 Henry Kenny was elected to the Dáil and served there for the next twenty-one years until he died from cancer.

'I think he took the same philosophy of playing Gaelic football into politics which was always to be fair to people. He was a very clean player and was never sent off. I think he only once got angry which was after Roscommon's Eamon Boland gave him a bit of "rough treatment". His only regret was that he never "mastered hurling".'

Tom McNicholas is the only survivor of the 1936 Mayo team. At ninety-four years of age he is still driving his car and his former career as a teacher is evidence in the clarity of his directions to his home. He retains vivid memories of that team and is best equipped to give an objective assessment of Henry Kenny.

'There wasn't the same cult of personality back then but there was no question that the star of our team was Henry. He was wonderful at catching balls in the air. He had great duels with the mighty Kerry midfielder Paddy Kennedy and was probably one of the very few players, if not the only footballer, who could hold his own with Kennedy. This was particularly the

case in the All-Ireland semi-final in Roscommon when we beat Kerry 1-5 to 0-6 in 1936 when Kennedy was the new star in the game.

'Henry was known as "the man with the magic hands". He had big hands and he could hold the ball in one hand. Now our game has become more like basketball there is so much hand-passing. Back then though it was a game of catch and kick and nobody did it better than Henry. I don't think he would believe the way the game has changed especially the emphasis on stopping teams from playing and, above all, the number of times people pass the ball backwards. Henry believed in positive football and playing your own game rather than the opposition's. We didn't have Man of the Matches then or dream teams but if there had been Henry would have won a lot of awards. I have often heard him described as Connacht's best midfielder. If there was one player from our team that could have made the Connacht team of the Millennium it would have been him.'

That team in full was:

1. Johnny Geraghty
(Galway)

2. Enda Colleran    3. Paddy Prendergast    4. Seán Flanagan
(Galway)    (Mayo)    (Mayo)

5. Brendan Lynch    6. Gerry O'Malley    7. Martin Newell
(Kerry)    (Roscommon)    (Galway)

8. Padraic Carney      9. Nace O'Dowd
(Mayo)      (Sligo)

10. Kevin Winston    11. Seán Purcell    12. Micheál Kearins
(Roscommon)    (Galway)    (Sligo)

13. Tony McManus    14. Tom Langan    15. Packy McGarty
(Roscommon)    (Mayo)    (Leitrim)

*Left:* The Fab Four (from left): Paddy Moclair, Patsy Flannelly, Henry Kenny and Purty Kelly.

# Lovely Leitrim

## Packy McGarty

Packy McGarty was born in Mohill in 1933 and his senior inter-county career began in 1949 and finished in 1971 when he was 39. He played in six senior Connacht finals without winning one of them and reached the National League semi-final in the spring of 1959. The closest he came to glory was when Galway beat Leitrim by 2-10 to 1-11 in the 1958 Connacht final. Although there was no question that McGarty was the star Leitrim had other good players at the time like Cathal Flynn at corner-forward. Football dominated Packy's life from an early age.

'Football was all you had. Every evening as a boy I'd go with my friends to see the men training. We'd be hoping that the ball would go over the bar and we'd be fighting just to get a kick of it. As kids we hadn't footballs just a sock with grass in it. You'd be listening to a match on a Sunday which was the highlight of the week because my father had fifteen shillings a week to keep a family of five of us. I remember working for three shillings a week.'

No one was more surprised than McGarty at his astonishingly quick elevation to inter-county status.

'I was selected for my first match for Leitrim when I was sixteen against Offaly and I didn't even know I was picked. A fella came to the door the day of my match and said: "Where's your stuff?"

"How do you mean?" I answered.

"You're playing today." I didn't believe him but eventually he persuaded me and it went OK and I got a couple of scores.'

It was the Railway Cups that brought McGarty his only national honours.

'We won the Railway Cup in 1957 and '58 and were beaten by a point in the final in 1959. I missed it because I was working in England and got a flu because of the smog. I was disgusted missing it because I loved playing with Seán Purcell and Frank Stockwell.

'That Galway team should have won the three-in-a-row after

*Above:* Packy McGarty shows he still has magic in his toes as he takes off on a solo run. *Photo:* Nicola Dihrberg

winning in 1956. They threw it away. Cork beat them by a point in the All-Ireland semi-final, mainly because the Galway midfield didn't play well on the day, only to lose the final to Louth. Galway were overconfident. They then played Louth in the League and hammered them! Then they lost the semi-final to Dublin in 1958 by a point after twice nearly smashing the crossbar with what should have been goals.'

McGarty won a third Railway Cup medal as a sub in 1967. He would have needed a trophy cabinet if the plethora of individual awards that we have today existed in his playing days.

'There was no such thing as All-Stars at the time. The closest thing was to be selected for Ireland˙to play against the Combined Universities. One year I played for Connacht in the Railway Cup final my opponent was the Kerry right-half back Seán Murphy who won five All-Ireland medals and was chosen in that position on the team of the century. The next day I played on him for Ireland against the Combined Universities. The following Friday evening I played on him for my club Seán McDermotts against UCD.'

Which was his most memorable match?

'The game I recall most was a Connacht Championship match against Sligo in 1956. I gave up everything to train for it: my work and holidays and everything. On the day I was as stiff as a board and I couldn't move. I should have been taken off but I wasn't. If I played well we'd have won because all the other lads played well and I was useless. We only lost by three points. Two months later I was playing in a factory league game and all the training paid off and I was running up and down the pitch like a gazelle.

'I told this story to John D. Hickey of the *Irish Independent* for a series he was doing called, "The game I most remember". They gave me three quineas for it. It was the only thing I ever got out of football!'

What was his best game then?

'In 1957 we beat Leinster in the Railway Cup semi-final in Ballinasloe. I was on four different men on that day. I began by marking Gerry O'Reilly of Wicklow who was taken off and Stephen White of Louth was switched over on me and later Jim McDonnell and Paddy Gibbons of Kildare. Cathal Flynn and I got the entire Connacht tally apart from two points scored by Seán Purcell. I couldn't do anything wrong on the day.

'I had my boots in great nick at the time and would never wear boots in a match unless I had worn them for about three months in training but as we were getting ready to travel to the match in Dublin I left my gear behind me outside the car and it was stolen. When we got to Ballinasloe Jack Mahon's brother, Paddy, said he would buy me a new pair of boots but there was a fella from Ballinasloe, Jack Wood, who had an old pair of boots that fitted me and I kicked around for a bit in them and they seemed OK. My Seán McDermotts clubmate Kevin Behan gave me a pair of old socks. Gerry O'Malley had an extra pair of togs which he loaned to me – so I went out with strange boots, togs and socks and I played the game of my life!

'After that game I had a very big head. It's very easy to get a swelled head but it can be taken off just as quickly. The following Sunday I played in a club match in north Dublin. I was playing on an unknown and he never gave me a kick of the ball! He was as hardy a bit of stuff as I ever played on but he never even got a trial for Dublin. I can tell you my head was pretty small after that game.'

McGarty was always a great thinker about the game and there was one occasion when Leitrim reaped the reward for this.

'George Geraghty of Roscommon was an All-Ireland Colleges Champion high-jumper. I vividly remember the first time I ever saw him play. He was selected for my club Seán McDermotts at midfield. Although I wasn't a big man I loved running for the ball and jumping and could reach a fair height. I was on the forty that day and I went up for the ball once and had my hand on it but somebody soared in like a bird and took it off me. It was my own teammate, George. I knew we were playing Roscommon the following Sunday in the Connacht Championship and we would be in big trouble because they had both George and Gerry O'Malley at midfield.

'The thing about Gerry was that if he had been blessed with a great shot he would have beaten you on his own. He'd catch everything and solo through the entire defence but his kick would as easily go wide as it could go over the bar. That's why I would always have picked him at centre-half-back.

'That whole week I spent thinking about how we would stop George because I knew we wouldn't be able to stop O'Malley no matter what plan we came up with. At half-time we were leading Roscommon by eight points to three and we had been playing with a bit of a breeze. Twenty minutes into the second half it was 8-8 and George and O'Malley were lording it at midfield. I decided to go to centre-field because we weren't in the game. I switched out on George because Gerry was like an octopus. I had a plan in my mind. As the ball was cleared out George was winning everything by running up and catching it so I would back into him and stop him running but when the ball was about to drop I'd sprint out and catch it. We won by eleven points to nine. The next morning the headline in the paper was, "Super Switch by Leitrim Wins Game". The thing was Leitrim didn't know a thing about it! I told George later that the biggest mistake he ever made was playing for Seán McDermotts the week before because I knew his form.

'I saw Pat Donnellan of Galway doing the same to Mick O'Connell once in an All-Ireland final and Mick didn't like it! It was effective but it wasn't dirty.

'I remember Colm O'Rourke writing an article explaining how Meath beat Cork in the All-Ireland replay in 1988 when Gerry McEntee was sent off early in the game. Their tactic was to foul an opponent out the field and then they were no longer a man down because a Cork player had to take the free. It was very effective but it was no way to win because it's much too negative and ruins the game as a spectacle.'

In 1984 McGarty was selected on the Team of the Century for players who never won an All-Ireland senior medal and fifteen years later was the only Leitrim payer chosen on the Connacht team of the Millennium. Probably the most revealing insight into McGarty's make-up comes when he is asked about the biggest regret of his career. It is not his failure to win even a Connacht medal as might have been expected.

'In one of my first matches with Leitrim when we played Cavan I was marking Brian O'Reilly. I gave him an elbow in the ribs. He just looked at me and said, "I play football." It was a lesson I never forgot about how to play the game and I've never felt so ashamed of myself.'

McGarty laughs heartily at the memory of an incident from his playing days. 'I went to America for the Kennedy games in 1964 with the late Charlie Gallagher and Gerry O'Malley. They were chalk and cheese but became amazingly close on the trip. O'Malley was very serious, religious and quiet. Charlie was devil-may-care. Every match he played he had to win. I played once with him in a veterans' match and he had to win that too! Gallagher was always winding Gerry up and saying that if they ever met in a match he would destroy him – which drove O'Malley mad. They were a pantomime. In private, Charlie admitted that he would have hated to have to play on O'Malley.

'Down's Joe Lennon was on that trip too. He had written a book about Gaelic football at the time and he brought loads of them out with him and sold them wherever he went. One day, Charlie went up to O'Malley and said, "You know what. I'm going to write my own book about football."

"Really! And I suppose we're going to see Gallagher on the front cover in full flight with the ball?"

"You will in my barney. You'll see a big, juicy blonde!"'

Packy's dream team from his own era is:

1. Johnny Geraghty
(Galway)

| 2. Jerome O'Shea | 3. Paddy Prendergast | 4. Tom O'Hare |
| (Kerry) | (Mayo) | (Down) |

| 5. Seán Murphy | 6. Gerry O'Malley | 7. Stephen White |
| (Kerry) | (Roscommon) | (Louth) |

8. Padraic Carney           9. Jim McKeever
(Mayo)                      (Derry)

| 10. Seán O'Neill | 11. Seán Purcell | 12. Paddy Doherty |
| (Down) | (Galway) | (Down) |

| 13. Denis Kelleher | 14. Tom Langan | 15. Kevin Heffernan |
| (Cork) | (Mayo) | (Dublin) |

# King of Yeats' County

## Micheál Kearins

Like so many players from the West of Ireland, Sligo's Micheál Kearins missed out on an All-Ireland medal. Micheál Ó Muircheartaigh furnished the definitive epitaph to Kearins's career, 'Some players are consistent. Some players are brilliant but Micheál Kearins was consistently brilliant.'

As a boy his hero was the great Sligo player Nace O'Dowd. Kearins first played for Sligo minors in 1960, losing out in the Connacht championship to a Galway side powered by Noel Tierney and Johnny Geraghty that went all the way to win an All-Ireland final. The following year he made his debut for the senior team against Cavan in a League game in Ballymote, and he played for the county at all three levels that year. In all, he played seventeen successive championship seasons with Sligo from 1962 to 1978. There were many disappointments along the way, notably losing the Connacht final to Galway in 1965, but he remains philosophical: 'My dedication and love of Gaelic football always keep me going.'

*Above:* Shoulder High: Sligo fans carry Micheál Kearins off Croke Park after a superlative display in the 1968 League semi-final against Kildare.

*Above:* Every breath you take: Micheál Kearins gets close attention from Roscommon's Pat Lindsay in the 1974 League semi-final replay. *Photo:* Tony Conboy

Micheál's place in the lore of Gaelic football is secure if only because of his phenomenal scoring feats, setting records that had no equivalent in the past and are not likely to find even an echo in the future. He was the country's leading marksman in competitive games in four different years: 1966, 1968, 1972 and 1973. In the drawn 1971 Connacht final he scored a record fourteen points, five from play and nine from placed balls. He won two Railway Cup medals during a thirteen-year career with Connacht, in 1967 and 1969. Two years later he scored twelve points for Connacht against the Combined Universities in the Railway Cup, all from placed balls. With the Combined Universities leading by 3-9 to 0-17, Connacht got a line ball 45 yards out in the dying seconds and Kearins slotted it over the bar to earn Connacht a replay. However, this is not the score that stands out the most in his memory. 'It was a sideline kick from thirty yards in the Connacht final of 1971 against Galway.'

His was a natural rather than a manufactured talent. Although he ranks with stars like Ollie Campbell as among the greatest place-kickers in the history of Irish sport, he did very little actual practice in that area. 'Especially in the early years I did a lot of physical training on my own – I would run a few miles early in the morning maybe four times a week. I never bothered practising my free-taking, not even taking a practice one in the kick-about before a match.'

His introduction to championship football in 1962 was the story of his career in shorthand: so near and yet so far. Sligo led by a point against the reigning champions, but Roscommon stole victory with a goal in the last kick of the game, and went on to contest the All-Ireland final.

Galway star Johnny Hughes perceptively observes: 'I often said if there had been a transfer system in Gaelic football and we could get just one of either Dermot Earley, Tony McManus or Micheál Kearins in the 1970s we would have won not one but three All-Irelands. All three would have stood out in any company.'

All through his long career Kearins never shed the burden of having the weight of Sligo fans' expectations resting on his shoulders. 'I was always nervous before a game, knowing Sligo people were depending on me. To slot the first free over was always very important to help me relax.'
He won an All-Star award in the inaugural year of 1971 at left-half-forward. He was also a replacement All-Star in 1972; indeed a major controversy ensued when he was omitted from the original selection. In 1984 he was 'greatly honoured' to be selected at left-half-forward on the Team of the Century for players who had never won an All-Ireland senior medal.

His first Railway Cup game was against Leinster in Ballinasloe. At the start, as he was moving into position before the ball was thrown in, he noticed his immediate opponent, Paddy McCormack, digging a hole along the ground with his boot.

McCormack said, 'You're young Kearins, from Sligo. I presume you expect to go back to Sligo this evening.'

'Hopefully,' Kearins replied.

'If you don't pass the mark, you have a fair chance of getting back.'

Paddy McCormack, the Iron Man from Rhode, was a tough man though the story goes that when he made his debut for Offaly his mother was concerned about the physical nature of the exchanges. She turned to her husband and said, 'Poor Paddy will break a leg.'

According to folklore her husband looked at her reproachfully and said, 'He might but it won't be his own.'

After a glittering career with Sligo, Kearins became a referee. As a referee he is probably best remembered for two games. In one, he controversially sent Meath star Colm O'Rourke off. 'It was an incident after half-time and he got a heavy shoulder while in possession. It knocked the ball out of his hands, but he didn't try to retrieve it; instead he came after me. He followed me the whole way down the field, sharing "pleasantries" with me! I had no option but to send him off.'

The two had another heated exchange subsequently, in the 1988 All-Ireland semi-final, when Kearins was a linesman.

'There was a line-ball incident and he felt that I gave the wrong decision. I know now, having seen the replay on the telly, that I was wrong and he was right. I would have to say, though, that he was a great player and made the Meath forward line tick while he was in his prime. He was their playmaker.'

The other controversial refereeing performance was during an All-Ireland semi-final between Cork and Dublin in 1989.

'I had to send Keith Barr off that day. Barr got involved in an incident five minutes earlier and he ran thirty or forty yards to get involved in that second incident. There was an awful lot of off-the-ball stuff that day and it's very hard to manage those games.' In fact the tension escalated to such an extent that Kearins publicly pulled the captains, Dinny Allen and Gerry Hargan, aside before the start of the second half and instructed them to warn their players about their behaviour. He didn't get exactly the response he hoped for from Allen who, when quizzed by the Cork lads about what the referee said, claimed Kearins had simply wished them well for the second half and hoped the awful weather would improve.

He selects a fellow West of Ireland man when asked about the greatest player he ever saw. 'It has to be Seán Purcell. He could play anywhere and had all the skills, Mick O'Connell's anticipation for fielding was great, too. My most difficult opponent, though, was Donegal's Brian McEniff.' Kearins' dream team is:

1. Johnny Geraghty
(Galway)

2. Donie O'Sullivan     3. Noel Tierney     4. Tom O'Hare
(Kerry)     (Galway)     (Down)

5. Páidí Ó Sé     6. Gerry O'Malley     7. Martin Newell
(Kerry)     (Roscommon)     (Galway)

8. Mick O'Connell     9. Jim McKeever
(Kerry)     (Derry)

10. Matt Connor     11. Seán Purcell     12. Pat Spillane
(Offaly)     (Galway)     (Kerry)

13. Mike Sheehy     14. Seán O'Neill     15. Paddy Doherty
(Kerry)     (Down)     (Down)

# SuperMac

## Tony McManus

One test of fame is when everybody knows you by your first name alone. No further identification is required. Throughout Roscommon Tony McManus is known simply as 'Tony' – just one testimony to his magnificent contribution to Roscommon football over eighteen years in the county jersey. When McManus won his sixth Connacht senior football medal in 1991 he joined Eamonn Boland and Bill Jackson as the only Roscommon men to achieve such a distinction.

In 1989 McManus won his only All-Star, which more accurately reflects the politics of the awards rather than his prodigious talents. He did have more trips to America as a replacement All-Star.

'One of my abiding memories of my career is of waiting in the airport for our bags on the way home and Harry Keegan was chatting with Mick Lyons. Tyrone's John Lynch was also on the trip. John had blonde hair, wore an ear-ring and tight jeans. As he collected his bag Mick turned to Harry and said: 'God be with the days when corner-backs were corner-backs!'

Those trips left an enduring legacy with McManus.

'I had a great relationship with the County Board all along. They looked after me very well when I was in College, giving me extra expenses above the normal and I remember while in College, going on two All-Star trips as a replacement and getting extra cash to help me. That was very fair and I treated them very fairly afterwards. I never put in for expenses in my latter years with Roscommon.

'One of the great characters of Roscommon football was Danny Burke, a team selector and a postman in Castlerea. Before one of our Connacht finals the announcer called out Danny's name instead of our star half-back Danny Murray. It got the biggest cheer of the day.

'In my early playing days we were against Armagh and at that stage if we went down injured, Danny Burke was the man who looked after you. Danny was a postman with no medical knowledge. Now, things are a lot

*Above:* Mac-nificent: Tony McManus bears down to goal against Cork in the All-Ireland semi-final in 1990. Roscommon midfielder John Newton (far right) is in support.
*Photo:* Roscommon Champion/*Gerard O'Loughlin*

more sophisticated with proper medical back-up. My brother Eamonn got a kick in the groin and Danny was in like a flash. After examining Eamonn carefully he said, "One, two, you're alright, they're still there"!'

McManus became a Championship regular in 1977 as Roscommon won the first of four consecutive Connacht titles.

'It was great to be a corner-forward with Dermot Earley at midfield. He hit a tremendous long ball to you on your outside, giving you the chance to win the ball.'

1978 would see one of the great days in recent Roscommon history.

'We beat Kerry in the Under-21 All-Ireland final. Kerry were very cocky and allowed us to play the match in Roscommon. I know it still rankles with some Kerry people that they conceded home advantage to us and made our task a lot easier. In the warm-up match our senior team had a rare victory over Kerry in the Ceannarus tournament so it was a very sweet memory for me.'

The disappointment of losing the 1980 All-Ireland to Kerry has never faded for McManus.

'I still feel aggrieved by the refereeing that day. It was outrageous. The ref was from Monaghan and I still have Monaghan people apologising to me for it. It seemed to us as if he had a preconceived idea that Kerry were destined to win and when it wasn't going according to the script that they had to get every decision their way.

'I am not one to hold a grudge but I still am annoyed by Mick O'Dwyer's reaction to it. He said nothing at the reception the next day but down in Kerry he said that dirty tactics would never beat Kerry. That still sticks in my throat. There was reference made to the treatment of John Egan. The implication was that Harry Keegan, who marked him in the final, was a dirty player. John would be the first to admit that Harry was not that sort of player. I think it is the only time that I ever saw Dermot Earley angry was at those comments. I felt that O'Dwyer conveniently overlooked a few tackles that our forwards had to take. Every time I went for the ball that day, I had my jersey pulled. I accept that as part and parcel of the game, but then to hear his comments after the match you would think that all the sinning was on one side and that Kerry were above reproach.

'I never had a problem with any of the Kerry lads. Myself and John O'Gara were very friendly with Ogie Moran, Bomber Liston and Mikey Sheehy. All of the Roscommon players got on very well with the Kerry lads apart from Pat Spillane.

'We were sick after losing but I thought I would be back again the next year and many times more afterwards. How wrong I was. Looking back the real one that got away was when we lost to Dublin in the semi-final the previous year, a game we should have won. We wouldn't have won that year but the experience of having been in a final would have helped us to win in 1980.'

The next years would be lean ones for Roscommon. McManus missed out on Roscommon's best chance to win their next Connacht final in 1986 when, through his work as a vet, he contracted brucellosis. More disappointment was to follow.

'We had a good side when we won the Connacht final in both '90 and '91. We had picked up good players. Paul Earley was excellent in those years. In '91 we played Meath in the All-Ireland semi-final. Meath were there for the taking. Again decisions went against us at crucial stages. It was a game we could have and should have won. That is the game that haunts me to this day.'

McManus is upbeat about the future of Roscommon football.

'When Feargal O'Donnell led the Roscommon minors to that famous All-Ireland title in 2006 he sowed a seed that will bear fruit in the next few years with the senior team. Some of those guys had a lot of potential.'

Tony played in five All-Ireland club finals with his beloved Clann na Gael, only to lose each of them.

'It was pretty devestating. I felt if we had won one we would have won a few but the mental block became too strong at the end. The game that still haunts me is the final we lost to St Finbarrs. I didn't have the best of games that day.'

Earlier in his career, club football had provided McManus with some of his happiest memories in the game during his time in UCD between 1976 and 1980.

'In 1979 I was captain and Colm [O'Rourke] was vice-captain. We became good friends. He was tremendously witty and sarcastic. Our coach Eugene McGee produced a newsletter about the fortunes of the team and he named the player who never shut up as the mouth of the team but he added that Colm was a strong contender! O'Rourke is very confident. The only time I ever saw him nervous was when I met him before the All-Ireland semi-final in 2007 when his son Shane was playing. He was never nervous when he played himself but he was that day.

'From our "Freshers" year Eugene had taken Colm and myself under his wing. He was a complex character but it was very enjoyable working with him. He certainly had a way with him. He commanded respect and had great ideas and was able to communicate them. There were lots of county players around at that time but he had no qualms about dropping them. Reputations meant nothing to him. You never knew what to expect from him. Days you thought you played well he might lacerate you. Days you thought you didn't pay well he would encourage you and compliment you.

'My lasting memory of him came the day we had to play Queens. The night before was the Veterinary Ball and I had gone. The next morning he heard about it and was not happy. He made me travel with him in his car and never said a word to me all the way up to Belfast. In the circumstances I was really keen to do well and I scored 2-3. He said nothing to me after the match. Eventually when all the lads were gone and I was behind waiting for him in the dressing room to make the journey home he turned to the caretaker and said in his typically gruff accent: "Would you have a jackhammer to widen the door a bit more? This fella's head is so big he won't be able to get out through it.'

As a prologue to selecting his dream team McManus singled out one player for special praise.

'Matt Connor was the best player I ever played with or against. At times I was in awe of his skill and class.'

McManus excluded Roscommon players from consideration in his dream team to prevent accusations of bias.

1. Martin Furlong
(Offaly)

| 2. Páidí Ó Sé | 3. Mick Lyons | 4. Seamus McHugh |
|:---:|:---:|:---:|
| (Kerry) | (Meath) | (Galway) |
| 5. Tommy Drumm | 6. Tim Kennelly | 7. Niall Cahalane |
| (Dublin) | (Kerry) | (Cork) |

8. Jack O'Shea          9. Brian Mullins
(Kerry)                 (Dublin)

| 10. Matt Connor | 11. Larry Tompkins | 12. Pat Spillane |
|:---:|:---:|:---:|
| (Offaly) | (Cork) | (Kerry) |
| 13. Colm O'Rourke | 14. Eoin Liston | 15. Mike Sheehy |
| (Meath) | (Kerry) | (Kerry) |

Captains Fantastic

# Captain Sensible

## Jimmy Murray

Y{ou only get one chance to make a first impression and I blew mine with Jimmy Murray. He stood on the sidelines as I made my club debut for St Brigids in an Under-12 match against his St Dominic's side. Suffice to say we were narrowly beaten – by 7-12 to 0-2 – and I was taken off at half-time!

I think the fact that he knew my grandfather, who died before I was born, cemented my affection for him. Born on 5 May 1917 Jimmy was a walking history book, recalling amongst other things the burning of his home village by the hated Black and Tans in 1921. The glory years of Roscommon football came in the 1940s. 'If we have the ball they haven't it' was their motto at the time. Murray's pub-cum-grocery in Knockcroghery, now run by Jimmy's son John, is arguably the spiritual home of Roscommon football with all its memorabilia from the county's All-Ireland successes in 1943 and 1944, both under the captaincy of Jimmy, including the football itself from the 1944 final. The football survived a close shave some years ago when Jimmy's premises were burned down – as he recalled to me with mixed feelings:

'The ball was hanging from the ceiling and of course the fire burned the strings and the ball fell down and rolled safely under the counter. The fire happened on a Saturday night and when the fire-brigade came one of the firemen jumped off and asked me, "Is the ball safe?" As I was watching my business go up in smoke the ball wasn't my main priority! But the fireman came out later with the ball intact. The next day I got calls from all over the country asking if the ball was safe. I was a bit annoyed at the time that all people seemed to be concerned with was the safety of the ball and nobody seem to be too bothered about what happened to the shop!'

As a boy, Jimmy was introduced to the magic of the GAA by the

*Preceding page:* Square Ball: Roscommon launch an attack on the Cavan goal in the 1943 All-Ireland final. Jimmy Murray, in the Number 11 jersey on the near right, gets special attention.

*Above:* Shoulder to Shoulder: Jimmy Murray is hoisted off the pitch after Roscommon win the 1943 All-Ireland. They defeated Cavan by 2-7 to 2-2 in a replay in front of over 47,000 spectators.

greatest evangelist since Matthew, Mark, Luke and John.

'Listening to the radio we never saw those great players but Micheál O'Hehir, who really made the GAA, turned them into superheroes. The first time I lined out in an All-Ireland final in 1943 and an hour before we got to Dublin I was nearly standing up just to get my first glimpse of Croke Park. That was my dream come true.

'One of my most vivid memories of my playing career is my brother Phelim telling me that the prince of midfielders Paddy Kennedy came over to him in the 1946 All-Ireland final and said: "Phelim, I think it's your All-Ireland." Phelim replied: "You never know, anything can happen, there's still over five minutes to go." Phelim's words were prophetic because Kerry

*Above:* The Roaring Forties: Jimmy Murray returns to Roscommon with the Sam Maguire Cup in 1944 after defeating Kerry 1-9 to 2-4 in front of a then record All-Ireland final attendance of 79,245 with many thousands waiting outside.

got two goals in the dying minutes to draw the game and they went on to win the replay.'

Why was his Roscommon team so successful?

'We had great players. Donal Keenan was one of the best men I ever saw to take a free. I saw him play one of his last matches of his career in Carrick-on-Shannon. Roscommon got a free along the sideline but it was an awful wet day. There was a long delay before the free was taken because of an injury to one of the players and they were throwing a coat on Donal to keep the rain off him and then he stepped up and slotted the ball between the posts. I said to myself, "That's some free."

'We also had some powerful men. Bill Carlos had legs like tree trunks. Brendan Lynch was like a tank. I remember reading an article by one of the greats of Mayo, Eamonn Mongey, which asked the question: Who is the toughest player in Ireland? His answer was Brendan Lynch. I mean hard but not dirty. You'd prefer not to be playing on him.'

Behind the scenes, Jimmy played a significant role in one of his Roscommon's most glorious triumphs. His message to the Roscommon minor team before the 2006 All-Ireland final was taken to heart: 'The will to win is the most important thing of all. There must be nothing else on your mind, only winning. Never think of getting beaten out there.'

He had mixed feelings about the changes in the game since his retirement. While he accepted that it is faster now, he was worried that the skills were not all that they might be. Like Pat Spillane he wanted to see the 'foot' come back into football.

A heavy cloud of sadness came over all GAA fans and players when they heard the news of Jimmy's death – he was universally acknowledged as one of Ireland's greatest footballers and captains. In his graveside eulogy for Jimmy, Dermot Earley quoted Seamus Heaney's words: 'The space we stood around has been emptied into us to keep.'

Jimmy Murray will forever remain a true GAA icon. It is an accolade earned by very few. The Sam Maguire trophy is a repository of secrets and dreams. Two of them are the best elegy. Memory is our way of holding on to those we love. Jimmy has left us a treasure trove of Croke Park memories. Jimmy, after considerable reluctance, selected this dream team. He prefaced his decisions with the following: 'Whenever I talk to GAA fans there were always great arguments about who had the best half-back line of all time: the Roscommon half-back line of 1943–4 with Brendan Lynch, Bill Carlos and my brother Phelim or the Cavan back line of 1947–8. I can still hear Micheál O'Hehir calling them out, "On the right is P. J. Duke, in the centre Commandant John Joe O'Reilly and on the left Lieutenant Simon Deignan." There have been so many great half-backs since so it is hard to select the best half-back line, never mind the greatest team of all time. There were so many great forwards too like Tom Langan and Seán Purcell and the list goes on and on.'

1. Danno Keeffe
(Kerry)

2. Enda Colleran        3. Paddy Prendergast        4. Seán Flanagan
(Galway)                    (Mayo)                          (Mayo)

5. Brendan Lynch        6. Bill Carlos        7. John Joe O'Reilly
(Roscommon)                (Roscommon)            (Cavan)

8. Mick O'Connell            9. Paddy Kennedy
(Kerry)                          (Kerry)

10. Mick Higgins        11. Seán Purcell        12. Padraic Carney
(Cavan)                    (Galway)                  (Mayo)

13. Seán O'Neill        14. Tom Langan        15. Kevin Heffernan
(Down)                    (Mayo)                    (Dublin)

# Like Father, Like Son

## Seán & Dermot Flanagan

B efore it became known as 'Angola' Seán Flanagan served as Minister in the Department of Health for three years (1966–69) and then served as Minister for Lands for four years (1969–73). He was elected to the European Parliament in 1979, having first been elected to the Dáil in 1951. However, his fame in Mayo resides chiefly for his achievements on the football field, which saw him captaining the county to All-Ireland titles in both 1950 and '51. He was selected at left-corner-back on both the Team of the Century and Team of the Millennium.

Even as a teenager in St Jarlath's College Flanagan showed his true colours on and off the field. He captained the school to its first Junior Championship only to discover that there was no cup to be presented. He improvised and borrowed a Golf Cup from one of the priests in the College. When he played for Connacht Colleges in 1939 he was involved in an early example of player power. The team suffered a bad beating and the manager, a priest, thought they had disgraced the province and refused to give them their jerseys. The players staged an immediate revolt on the basis that they had tried their best and held a sit-in the team hotel until they got their way. When the priest said: 'I give you my word of honour as a priest,' one of the players showing untypical lack of reverence for the clergy for the times replied: 'We need your word of honour as a man.' Victory went to the players at least in the argument.

Things were also tense when Flanagan began to play for Mayo. Relations with the county board were less than harmonious. Such was Flanagan's frustration with the incompetence of the County Board that he resigned from the team in 1947. The county secretary, Finn Mongey, wrote back to say he had placed his letter before the Board, who asked him to reconsider, and make himself available for the '48 season. The League was beginning in Tralee but Flanagan said he would not travel. Following intense moral pressure from his friend and teammate Eamonn 'George' Mongey, he was eventually persuaded to go. When the team reached Tralee, Flanagan

*Above:* Jack's back: Seán Flanagan has Jack Lynch for company at a Fianna Fáil Ard Fheis in 1979 with the first European elections looming.

was addressed by a man who asked him in which position he played. When Flanagan told him he was a corner-back the man said in a strong Kerry brogue: 'Aren't you a bit small to play full-back? Kerry always have great backs, big strong men.' Flanagan's blood was boiling and retorted: 'Mayo came here in 1939 and we beat the lard out of you. We propose to do the same to you tomorrow.'

The incident did not so much light a flame under Flanagan as much as a powder keg. All his hesitancy was vanquished. The Kerry game had become a do-or-die issue for him. Although Mayo had only fifteen players, they drew with the Kerry men who had contested the historic All-Ireland final the previous year in the Polo Grounds in New York. Mayo were so desperate that the only subs they could tog out were the county secretary and the rather rotund team driver. The situation could not be left unchallenged. Flanagan and the established players on the team drafted a letter that left no room for ambiguity.

'Year after year we have seen the County Board bring to nought the hours of training which we have put in, but yet, believing it was outside our sphere as players, we have desisted from drawing your attention to the matter. Events in Tralee last Sunday have banished our indecision, however, and we feel the time has come when something must be done before football disappears completely in Mayo – unwept, unhonoured and unsung.'

Mayo secured two Connacht titles but they failed to win the All-Ireland. A view emerged within the more progressive elements of the County Board that Sam would not return to Mayo until Flanagan was made

*Above:* A team of all talents: The Connacht Railway Cup team of 1952. 'The Flying Doctor' Padraic Carney (front row – third from right) is between Seán Flanagan (fourth from right) and Paddy Prendergast. Tactical genius Eamonn Mongey (second from left) joins Roscommon great Gerry O'Malley (first on left). The back row contains the two Connacht forwards selected on the GAA Team of the Millennium, Tom Langan (fourth from right) with Seán Purcell on his right.

captain. The problem was that Flanagan 'only' played for a junior team. This required a change of rule at the Convention giving the captaincy of the senior team to the nominee of the county champions. Flanagan duly repaid the County Board for their benevolence by immediately banning them from any contact with the team until after they had won the All-Ireland! He did make an exception for the Chairman of the County Board and the County Secretary Finn Mongey. One other member, a man of the cloth, thought he should be an exception and paid a visit to the team during their collective training. Flanagan was over to him immediately and coolly informed him: 'Get out and I'll see you when I have the Sam Maguire.' While this did nothing for his popularity, winning the next two All-Irelands did surmount any residual problems in that area.

• • • • • • • • •

Dermot Flanagan spent his early years on the Mayo side of Ballaghaderreen. 'So split is the town between Roscommon and Mayo that I joke that even

*Above:* The Blessed Trinity: three of the stars of Mayo's finest team (from left): Seán Flanagan, Fr Peter Quinn and Eamonn Mongey in Maynooth in 1953.

the marital bed could come under pressure when the two counties meet in the Connacht Championship.' The family moved to Dublin when he was still in primary school. With the encouragement of his father he played a lot of soccer in his new home of Clontarf, one time even playing against Ronnie Whelan.

'I think I brought some of my soccer training into my Gaelic football. I was the first to pass the ball back to the goalkeeper which was considered very avant garde at the time.'

Burdened with the 'son of' syndrome Flanagan was self-conscious in his teenage years about his place on the pitch. Such was the extent of his angst about this that he chose to play as a half-forward rather than as a defender. When he was seventeen he decided to declare for Mayo minors, which was unusual at the time for a player living in Dublin. It was only after he went to UCD in 1979 and Eugene McGee drafted him in as a half-back, that he found his position as a defender, before finally settling in to his father's old role at left full-back.

It is immediately apparent in conversation with him that he has intimate knowledge of the innermost workings of his father's mind and his thoughts on the team. He is prey to the secrets of its success.

'Eamonn Mongey did everything to a very high standard and had a single-minded approach. Paddy Prendergast mightn't have been the tallest full-back but he had a spring in his step like Willie Joe Padden and could soar in the air. Mongey and Padraic Carney had a tremendous partnership. The entire team were great players individually who would all be superstars today and collectively they were a wonderful unit. When the going got tough, they had the ability to come through really difficult games. They never knew when they were beaten. For them it wasn't just about football. Times were tough. They really wanted to do something that transcended the harshness of life and give Mayo people something they could never get in ordinary life.'

Likewise, Dermot is keenly aware of his father's place in the drama.

'He was part of a great full-back unit. Mongey and my dad were very big on strategy and tactics. Dad was always thinking ahead. Before the 1951 All-Ireland for some reason the Meath players had to walk through the Mayo dressing room in Croke Park. Dad had warned his players that none of them were to make eye contact with the Meath lads because he wanted to make a statement that Mayo meant business.'

In 1982, having just established himself on the Mayo team, Flanagan found himself training with Dublin's Kerry-based players. In the best GAA tradition this was an accidental by-product of a controversy. Micheál Ó Muircheartaigh was training players like Mick Spillane and Jack O'Shea in UCD but a newspaper made a big issue of the fact that none of the players involved were attending UCD. A Gaelic football solution to a Gaelic football problem had to be found. As secretary of the UCD club Flanagan wrote and invited the Dublin-based Kerry footballers to join the UCD players involved in summer training.

'Micheál was very welcoming. The first night he pointed to me and said to the Kerry lads: "You'll see that man winning an All-Ireland." I deeply appreciated his comments. His training methods were very modern and sophisticated. When I went back to train with Mayo I was noticeably sharper because the training was so crisp. The big thing for me was that in March they were training for September whereas counties like Mayo were only training in four week bursts until the next match. Psychologically I found that the Kerry way made you believe you were an All-Ireland contender rather than hoping you might possibly be one.'

Flanagan holds a unique, albeit poignant, distinction among all players. 'I was the last person to mark Offaly's Matt Connor before his horrific accident. He would've been one of my heroes.'

In 1985 Mayo reached the All-Ireland semi-final against Dublin. Flanagan's background was to prove a mixed blessing in the run-up to the match.

'There was a lot of media attention on me before the game because I was the only link to the '50 and '51 teams and that drained me, in the first half of the first game I was feeling the effects.'

Nonetheless his performance on Barney Rock in the replay, keeping him scoreless from play, helped Flanagan to win the first of his two All-Stars that year. His next semi-final against Meath in 1988 was at once memorable and unremembered.

'It was a very physical game and I was knocked unconscious. I almost swallowed my tongue and was a little perturbed to find out afterwards that I could have died.'

The promise of reaching the All-Ireland final in 1989 was not built on and Flanagan looks back on the experience as a lost opportunity.

'The winter of '89 saw a form of euphoria because we had reached a final after such a long time and had played well which really took away from our focus. What should have happened is that we should have cleared off for a week and realised we had lost. People thought we were on the crest of winning an All-Ireland, which created a lot of distractions and left us vulnerable in '90.'

To this day Flanagan finds if difficult to assess the way events unfolded after Mayo's defeat in the Connacht final replay to Roscommon in 1991.

'John O'Mahony departed in controversial circumstances. John has never spoken in public about all the details and I suppose we should let him have his say on that. It is probably fair to say that part of the reason was that he was not allowed to choose his own selectors. Looking back the circumstances of Mayo football were not right then.

'Brian McDonald came in as his replacement and a year later would find himself in a huge controversy. Were there any winners? Everybody was a loser to a greater or lesser extent. Brian had been a selector with Liam O'Neill in 1985. To be fair to Brian he had a lot of good ideas about the game but whether he was the man to get the best out of players was another question. The first thing he asked me when he took over as manager was if I was committed to Mayo football. I was totally committed. I was the first guy to do stretching before training and after training. Long before it was fashionable I was doing acupuncture, watching my diet, reading sports injury books and doing power weight lifting – anything that would give me an edge or improve me as a player so it came as a shock to be asked that.

*Above:* Back off: Dermot Flanagan beats Roscommon's Derek Duggan to the ball in the 1991 Connacht final replay.

'The issue that got into the media was about the players pushing cars as part of a training session. That was not the underlying problem. You needed to have a very strong skin to be able to handle Brian's comments in a training session. That was OK for the senior players but repeated exposure to this for the younger players could have undermined their confidence. We had a lot of younger players in the squad at the time.

'Again, in fairness to Brian, we did win a Connacht final in 1992 and could have beaten Donegal in the All-Ireland semi-final. We were not in the right frame of mind for an All-Ireland semi-final. There were a lot of problems with organisation. I was a man marker and I was on Tony Boyle for a short time in the game and did well on him but I wasn't left on him and he played havoc with us.

'Afterwards the controversy broke in the media. The team was going nowhere. There were no winners in that situation. The tumultuous saga reflected very badly on the whole scene in Mayo. The County Board had been deaf to any complaints. John O'Mahony had left under a cloud. These situations don't come from nowhere. A lot of mistakes were made.' The sins of the father were revisited on Flanagan.

'My dad wouldn't have been hugely popular with the County Board in his playing days. One day he turned around and asked the County Chairman if he wouldn't mind leaving the dressing room. For that reason some people believed that I was the most likely instigator of the "revolt" against Brian but I had nothing to do with it. I never had to push cars because I was training in Dublin and was too busy in my legal career to be "masterminding a coup".'

It was hoped that Jack O'Shea's appointment as manager would revive Mayo's fortunes but it was not to be.
'We were very lucky to beat Roscommon in the Connacht final in 1993. I picked up a cruciate ligament injury and had to decide whether to retire or have surgery knowing that it might not be a success.'

John Maughan's appointment as Mayo manager would usher in a new era for Mayo football. Having recovered from his operation Flanagan was happy to know he was not forgotten.

'I really wanted to get involved again not just because of John but because of his backroom team of Peter Ford and Tommy O'Malley. Peter rang to invite me back. I told him I was going on holiday for two weeks in Portugal. I told my wife I was going back to play for Mayo so I spent the two weeks running up and down sand dunes. It was a huge psychological challenge for me. I was thirty-four and in the winter of my career. I knew the media scrutiny of me would be much greater to see if I had become a "has-been". I played in a challenge game against Donegal and Peter told me I had done fine. I was then selected to play against Galway in the League and that night Peter rang me to say that people had come to bury me but I had proved them wrong. I knew though that there would be ongoing questioning of whether I was the weak link on the Mayo team.'

It is clear from the tone of his voice that Flanagan still nurses a sense of frustration of one aspect of the events of 1996.

'We played some super football that year and were tremendous when we beat Kerry in the semi-final. Not winning the All-Ireland that year remains the big disappointment of my career. I am convinced that we were hard done by and I'm not just talking about the sending off of Liam McHale. Pat McEnaney – the referee – had come down to us before the final and had talked about what might happen if there was a shemozzle. I found his comments very strange and was convinced that there could be a very

serious incident in the game. People may think this is sour grapes but I still believe that the referee's decisions influenced the outcome of the game.'
Flanagan has a more personal regret about the loss to Kerry in the All-Ireland final in 1997.

'I had got a nick in my hamstring ten days before the final as had Maurice Sheridan. Both of us thought we were good enough to do a job but neither of us lasted the match. The ironic thing was that psychologically I never felt better in my head for the game. I had taken a month off work and was really psyched. There was no point of me going in for just five minutes if that's all I thought I could last – which is all I did. It is a huge regret of mine that I never got to contribute more to the team that day.'

Since his retirement, Flanagan has had ample time to appraise his career. 'Eugene McGee once asked me: "Why don't you play gobshite football?" I didn't understand what he meant then but I do now. I was fortunate that John O'Mahony asked me to be Mayo captain when he became manager. I had the job for over a year and I learned a lot about how not to be a captain. I took on too much worrying about everyone else's game when I should have just led by example. I would have liked the opportunity to have two or three years to grow into the role. What pleases me most is that the Mayo supporters came to respect me as Dermot Flanagan and not just the son of a famous footballer of the past.'

When I asked about his dream team, Flanagan said the team he would have liked to see playing the most was his father's Mayo All-Ireland winning team.

The 1950–01 Mayo team was:

1. Seán Wynne

2. John Forde      3. Paddy Prendergast      4. Seán Flanagan

5. Peter Quinn      6. Henry Dixon      7. John McAndrew

8. Padraic Carney      9. Eamonn Mongey

10. Mick Flanagan      11. Billy Kenny      12. Joe Gilvarry

13. Mick Mulderrig      14. Tom Langan      15. Peter Sloan

# Days of Grace

## Enda Colleran

Croke Park on All-Ireland final day is sacramental, a transcendental experience that calls automatically upon systems of thinking and feeling with a whole undergrowth of behaviour and sentiment and attitude. It satisfies so much in GAA folk that pine consciously or unconsciously for appeasement: a worthy stop-off on an unfinished and unfinishable journey for heroic feats. Few people were more attuned to its unique magic than the late Enda Colleran, who captained Galway to All-Ireland triumphs in both 1965 and 1966.

His first taste of All-Ireland success in 1964 was shrouded in sadness.

'After half-time, John Donnellan and I were walking out together. John was right-half-back and I was right-full. He turned to me and he said: "I think there's a row in the stand." In one portion of the stand there was an awful lot of people moving around and I said to him: "There must be." We didn't take any more notice at all. We played the second half and we won. We were in such good form but I noticed our officials were very subdued where they came in.

'We went into the dressing room after all the presentations. John said: "I want to go out to show the cup to the old man." Up to that they couldn't get an opportunity to take him aside and tell him. At that stage they had to tell him and then everybody changed. Actually, it wasn't a row at half-time but John's father had passed away in the stand. John's father had captained Galway and was a fantastic footballer. He died that day.

'It's amazing really, you think that an All-Ireland is the most important thing but everything changed, the atmosphere was totally subdued as you would expect. The next evening the Sam Maguire Cup was brought home in a funeral cortege rather than with a blaze of glory as is the norm. In fact Mick Higgins, who played on the same team as him, was actually watching the game at home and he collapsed and died as well. According to "rumour" when Mick Donnellan went to heaven when he died, and when he reached at the gates St Peter said to him: "Who won the All-Ireland?"

And he said: "Well, when I was leaving Galway were winning well but Mick Higgins will be up soon and he'll have the final score."'

Enda had no hesitation when I asked him his outstanding personal memory from the three-in-a-row triumph:

'It was the All-Ireland semi-final against Down in 1965, my best ever game. The ironic thing was that I had a terrible start to the match. I was marking Brian Johnson and he scored two points off me in the first few minutes. I felt that if I didn't get my act together he would end up as man of the match and decided to change my tactics. Down were storming our goal for most of the second half and I found that no matter where I went, the ball seemed to land into my hands. I seemed to be in the right place all the time and made all the right decisions. Often I took terrible decisions and went forward and left my man and still the ball came to me. I was so thankful that a thing like that happened to me in an All-Ireland semi-final rather than in a challenge game with two men and a dog watching.

'At one stage Seán O'Neill had the ball around the midfield and Paddy Doherty, completely unmarked, came at speed to the full-forward position. I had two options: one was to stay on my own man and the other was that Seán O'Neill would pass the ball to Paddy Doherty. I took the chance and ran for Paddy Doherty, and Seán O'Neill passed the ball to him and I actually remember coming behind Paddy trying not to make any noise, so that he wouldn't hear me coming towards him and at the last

*Below:* The Stamp of Greatness: Enda Colleran (right) with Pat Spillane at the launch of the Team of the Millennium stamps at Croke Park in 1999.

second I nipped in front of him and got possession. I felt he had a certain goal, only for that. It's amazing with sixty thousand people present, that I still thought my approach had to be as quiet as possible.'

A more tense occasion came the following year when Galway were to face the favourites Meath in the All-Ireland. Colleran was due to mark sprint champion Ollie Shanley, who had given a top class performance in the semi-final.

'Everybody was saying to me, "You've an awful job in the final to mark him, you'll never mark him." Martin Newell and I went out to the Aran Islands for a few days, just before we started training for the All-Ireland final and we were sleeping in the one room; he was on one side and I on the other. He woke up at one stage of the night and I was standing over him. I was sleep walking! Martin told me the next day that I said: "By Jaysus, if I can keep up with Shanley, I'll mark him." It just shows you the pressure I was under.'

What was the secret of Galway's success? 'We had great players individually but we were also a great unit. Likewise Mick O'Dwyer's Kerry was a team with all the roles. The teams that are most successful are the teams that mould as a team. If a team has one or two great players you can always blot them out and you can take them but you can't blot out six class forwards. You couldn't single out any one player on that Kerry side. They were a team of stars.

*Below:* Their cup runneth over: Enda Colleran (right) with Gary Fahy, Galway's All-Ireland winning captain, at the homecoming for the victorious All-Ireland team in 2001.

'We had great belief which meant that we would always believe we would win a game when it was tight at the end. Other teams choked in that position.

'We also had that vital ingredient you need if you are to win anything, that bit of luck. I think back especially to the Connacht Championship in 1965. Both Sligo and Mayo should have beaten us. It was there for them if they kept their heads. We were in terrible trouble against Sligo after they got two early goals but we just sneaked victory by three points. Against Mayo we were losing by a point in the dying minutes when they got a fifty. Three Mayo players were fighting over who should take it when one of them rushed up and kicked it straight to one of our half-backs. He cleared it up the field and we got the equalising point. And then we got the winning point almost immediately. Mayo were all over us that day and, without doubt, should have won. It's amazing how a tiny incident can make all the difference in deciding who gets their hands on the Sam Maguire Cup.'

Enda enjoyed the characters of Gaelic football: 'Offaly's Paddy McCormack was a great character and had a reputation as the Iron Man of Rhode. Mind you I saw someone putting it up to him once, who I won't name, and it wasn't so obvious who was the iron man!'

I was shocked to hear of Enda's sudden death in 2004 because to meet him one could not but be impressed by his fitness and vitality. In his case death was not the extinguishing of the light, but putting out the lamp because a new dawn had come. No doubt he is currently picking his own Best of the West team with Seán Purcell, Mattie McDonagh and Jimmy Murray on the playing fields of heaven. The dream team he selected for me was:

1. Johnny Geraghty
(Galway)

2. Donie O'Sullivan     3. Noel Tierney     4. Paddy McCormack
(Kerry)              (Galway)             (Offaly)

5. John Donnellan     6. Kevin Moran     7. Martin Newell
(Galway)             ( Dublin)              (Galway)

8. Mick O'Connell       9. Mattie McDonagh
(Kerry)                   (Galway)

10. Matt Connor     11. Seán Purcell     12. Pat Spillane
(Offaly)              (Galway)             (Kerry)

13. Mike Sheehy     14. Seán O'Neill     15. Liam Sammon
(Kerry)              (Down)              (Galway)

# Murphy's Law

## Barnes Murphy

As a boy Barnes Murphy had a confused sense of identity. 'I only found out I was from Sligo when I started secondary school in Saint Nathy's College in Ballaghaderreen. Because we grew up on the Mayo border and got the *Western People* every week I knew more about Mayo football than Sligo.'

At Nathy's, Murphy became lifelong friends with a man he would line out against many times in the years to come.

'Our star was Dermot Earley though in his first match we lost by 7-7 to 0-0. He hasn't changed one iota since then. As a result of going to school with him I always felt I could hold my own against him. In a match he would often get a dig in the ribs but he would never hit you back. The most he would ever do would be to ask you why you did it.'

The player though who had the most formative influence on Murphy's career was Sligo football's most famous son.

'I thought all my Christmasses had come at once when I first played for Sligo in 1967. When I was twelve I first saw Micheál Kearins play for Sligo and to be on the same team as him was a great thrill. I was advised to mark him in training. It was a f**king nightmare! He would dummy on the left side, then the right side but if you spent a year to two buying dummies from him you became a good marker. The experience definitely developed me as a player.'

1968 was a turning point in Sligo's fortunes.

'We qualified for a National League semi-final but we lost in a replay to Kildare. Nonetheless that was a big step forward for us and gave us a lot of confidence. That year Sligo minors also qualified for the All-Ireland minor final and many of the players came through to the senior team. We got more than most from that team. We came close in Connacht in the early '70s and in a League final. I especially remember a League semi-final against Offaly because it was a rare off day for Mickey with his frees but we still ran them close. A week later we played together for Connacht in

49

*Above:* Brilliant Barnes: Barnes Murphy (on right of picture) clears the ball for Sligo against Mayo in the Connacht final replay in 1975.

the Railway Cup final. Mickey was kicking frees for fun and scored thirteen points. After the game [Offaly star] Kevin Kilmurray came over to us and said: "Jaysus, Mickey, if you were kicking frees like that last week ye would beat us handy." Micheál told me: "Barnes I don't give a sh*t about today but the last day I tried everything I could but couldn't get the blady ball to go over the bar".'

In 1974 Roscommon needed a replay to beat Sligo in a National League semi-final. Murphy was rewarded for a string of fine performances through the year with an All-Star award. The trip had an unintended side effect.

'Getting an All-Star really meant a lot to me and it was a great to get to meet Kevin Heffernan and his team on that tour. I feel that the GAA owes them a lot. Gaelic football was not fashionable before them but they did a massive PR job for the game as was seen in the number of Dublin jerseys being worn at the time, which later spread to Mayo jerseys, Sligo jerseys and so on. That helped us in Sligo enormously in 1975. We need Dublin to win an All-Ireland every decade because of the hype they generate.'

On that tour Murphy befriended a man who, in west of Ireland parlance, was 'a horse of a footballer'.

'I remember Galway's Billy Joyce was a replacement on that team. I thought he was an awful so and so and he thought the exact same about

*Above:* Managerial Moment: Barnes Murphy (on the right) watches Sligo from the sideline as they play Roscommon in the 1981 Connacht Championship.

me! As a result we didn't even talk to each other at Shannon before flying out. On the trip, though, I got to know him very well and I found out he's the soundest guy ever and great fun. Billy and the Galway lads on the trip like Johnny Hughes and Tom Naughton said to me that Sligo always put it up to Galway for fifty minutes but Galway knew they would always take us in the last ten minutes. I was coaching the Sligo team at the time and after hearing these comments a number of times I was really fired up that was going to stop and when I got home I passed that fierce drive on to the rest of the team.

'When we played Galway in the Connacht Championship in 1975 every time Billy Joyce went for the ball I shouted "Judy" because that was the name of Billy's love interest at the time. He got more and more annoyed and once he shouted back to me: "If you don't shut up, I'll go back and hit you in the lug." I was delighted because it showed he was distracted from the game. In the end we won easy enough and then went on to win a Connacht final at last.'

As coach and captain Murphy saw the euphoria generated by the victory as a mixed blessing.

'We had three weeks to get ready then for Kerry in the semi-final. I am a non-drinker but for the first week I couldn't get some of the fellas to keep their heads out of drinking from the Nestor Cup. I was marking Mike

Sheehy and he wasn't getting a kick of the ball then he had to be replaced. I gave out to our corner-backs who gave Mike a belt because he wasn't doing us any damage. Instead his replacement came on and scored a goal. We were in the match until the second half of the second half. Kerry got three goals and two points in the last ten minutes.'

The match was to take on a deeper significance for Murphy personally than he had anticipated.

'As coach that year I had got both Brian McEniff and Tull Dunne to give us some help. Brian, for instance, had suggested that we change Micheál Kearins' style of play to get him to involve more of the forwards rather than take on everything himself. When I said this to Micheál he did not look happy and walked away but he started to do it in games. At the semi-final I asked Brian and Tull to keep an eye on things for me. I had been surprised when they didn't come into the dressing room at half-time but found out that they advised the Sligo selectors to make some changes but were rebuffed. The result of their attempts was shown just before we played our first game in the league that October. The county chairman came into the dressing room and said: "Now, lads, I would like you to introduce you to your new captain." That was the first time I had any indication that I was to lose the captaincy and my role as coach. I got such a shock. I didn't say anything but I was very annoyed.'

Despite the personal disappointment Murphy did not allow his commitment to his county to wane.

'I got married on Thursday the ninth of January in 1976 but didn't go on honeymoon because we were playing Galway the following Sunday. Apart from Micheál Kearins we had a very young side and I felt that if we had continued on the same way we could have built on our success but instead we went backwards. Thankfully we had great success at club level with St Marys, including winning an All-Ireland seven-a-side title in 1980. 'I was brought back to manage Sligo in 1980 and 1981. We beat Roscommon in the Connacht Championship in '81 even though they had contested the All-Ireland final the previous year. I brought myself on for the last few minutes. It was the only way I could get a game!'

Murphy has one regret from his playing days with Sligo.

"What we lacked was a player like Eamonn O'Hara. Take his goal in the Connacht final in 2007, which was one of the best goals I have ever seen. Everybody noticed his run and the rocket of a shot but what many

*Left:* Come to me: Barnes Murphy (on left) soars to claim the ball against Kerry in the 1975 All-Ireland semi-final despite the very close attention of Kerry midfielder Pat McCarthy.

people didn't notice was the great run he made for the ball. He plays a brand of football that I love. If we had a player like him, we would have won a lot more games in the 1970s.'

There is one Sligo player who is most associated with Murphy.

'A lot of people know the story of Micheál Kearins' first game with Connacht, marking Paddy McCormack. What they don't know is the postscript. Mickey was switched off Paddy and Cyril Dunne went on his place. Cyril went up to Paddy and said immediately: "Watch yourself or I'll give you a box." Paddy was very quiet for the rest of the game.

'Micheál had a serious side and a funny side. We were travelling to a match one day and Micheál, unusually, was coming on the team bus with us. It was often said that Sligo were a one-man team. Someone asked Micheál how the team were going. He replied: "I'm feeling great today!"

'In 2008 Micheál had a confrontation with a bull and the bull won. Micheál has put on a bit of weight since his playing days and when a friend of mine heard the news he rang me to inquire if the bull was OK!'

Murphy's dream team from his playing days is:

1. Billy Morgan
(Cork)

2. Willie Casey     3. John Brennan     4. Robbie Kelleher
(Mayo)            (Sligo)            (Dublin)

5. Seán Murphy     6. T. J. Gilmore     7. Pat Reynolds
(Kerry)            ( Galway)           (Meath)

8. Ray Carolan            9. Dermot Earley
(Cavan)                 (Roscommon)

10. Frank McGuigan     11. Colm McIllarney     12. Micheál Kearins
(Tyrone)            (Down)            (Sligo)

13. Matt Connor     14. Willie McGee     15. John Egan
(Offaly)            (Mayo)            (Kerry)

He chose these subs: Martin Furlong, Nicholas Clavin, Tom O'Hare, Páidí Ó Sé, Mick O'Connell, Brian Mullins, Eamonn O'Hara, Tony McManus and Jimmy Duggan.

# Mr Darcy

## Declan Darcy

Declan Darcy should have been another Ross O'Carroll-Kelly. Growing up in Sandymount in the heart of Dublin 4, an inhospitable, even barren, hinterland for the GAA, it was difficult to foresee that he would become the face of Leitrim football's finest hour. The fact that both his parents were from Leitrim was the catalyst for his immersion into club football in the county, though initially the move was shrouded in controversy.

'I was playing illegally with Aughawillian. I was not living or working there but I put my father's home place down as my address. Some people in other clubs didn't want me because I was giving Aughawillian an advantage but it was arranged by the club for me to play with Leitrim and that certainly made things easier. The great thing about playing with Aughawillian was that I found myself playing in big club tournaments at the age of sixteen or seventeen, like playing in a final in Cavan against Navan O'Mahonys up against Joe Cassells, Finian Murtagh and David Beggy which was surreal for me.'

A senior inter-county debut soon followed.

'I made my debut against Fermanagh wearing some ridiculous thing on my nose, having broken it just beforehand in a hockey match. I then played against Offaly. I started at wing-forward and was doing OK but then moved to centre-half-back. Every ball seemed to come to me then and I was the hero of the day and that was where I lined out from then on.'

Darcy soon learned an important footballing lesson.

'I was marking Greg Blaney in a Railway Cup. I was just a nipper and because I respected him so much I was marking him very tightly and hanging on to him for dear life. Eventually he lifted me with an elbow and it was lights out. I couldn't see a thing. Greg is a dentist but he knocked out two or three of my back teeth! He remembers the incident well and we've often laughed about it since. It taught me an invaluable lesson that when you are marking a top player you can't be hanging out of him. Finbarr Cullen famously found out the same thing marking Paul Curran. I learned

*Above:* Declan Darcy (front row: fourth from left) sits pensively. Mickey Quinn (back row: second from left) is psyched and ready for action before the 1994 semi-final.

that day that you don't cross the line and the next time I played on Greg I marked him very differently.'

Darcy's early years with Leitrim coincided with a significant upturn in the county's fortunes.

'Things started to roll when we beat red hot favourites Mayo, managed by John O'Mahony, in a Connacht Under-21 semi-final and then Galway in the Connacht final. Aughawillian were doing well and should have beaten Clann na Gael to win a Connacht title in the famous "battle of the fog". The bandwagon really developed when P. J. Carroll took over the management of the county side. At one stage we were playing a League match in Antrim. A special train from Dublin was run for Leitrim fans and ten or twelve coaches from the county came to the game. That level of support gave you energy when you went back to training the next Tuesday and created a great buzz. Looking back now, though we didn't realise it at the time, we were giving the county a great lift in the dark days of the early '90s. It was heartwarming stuff.'

Things moved up another gear when John O'Mahony became county manager.

'The first thing was that he came. Before he did he had seen us play when he was Mayo boss and we beat them out the gate in Carrick-on-Shannon so he knew what we could do. When he agreed to manage us we knew that he was coming because he believed something was going to happen.'

O'Mahony's midas touch worked its unique magic in 1994. One of the iconic images of the year was Darcy, as captain of the Connacht champions, holding the Nestor Cup with Tom Gannon who captained

*Above (left):* Shaking all over: Declan Darcy greets Dublin captain John O'Leary before the 1994 All-Ireland semi-final. *(right):* Winning can build a bridge: Declan Darcy at the presentation of the Nestor Cup in 1994 with Tom Gannon (wearing glasses), the only other Leitrim man to captain Leitrim to a Connacht title.

Leitrim to their only previous Connacht title in 1927. That was the start of an unforgettable adventure.

'I stayed in the Bush Hotel in Carrick the night after the game. The next morning the receptionist apologetically rang me and said she was being hounded by somebody who wanted to speak with me on the phone. I asked: "Who is it?"

"Pat Kenny."

I thought somebody was winding me up but sure enough it was Pat who came on the line and asked: "Where are you?"

"I'm in bed."

"With who?"

"With the Nestor Cup."

'After the interview I went out on the main street and was surprised at how quiet it was. I had expected a bit of a buzz. I went across the road to the pub and when I opened the door it was like a night club. The place was jammed and hyper and it was only 10.30 in the morning and Shannonside radio were broadcasting live in the corner.

'My abiding memory of the whole thing came that day in Ballinamore. When my father was asked where he was from he had always said, "West of the Shannon" rather than Leitrim. We did a tour of the county and it was very special. All the players went to their own clubs. The emotion was unbelievable but as someone who grew up in Dublin 4, I didn't have that local base. I found myself on the stage in Ballinamore not sure what to do when my father ran on, grabbed the cup and threw it in the air like a mad lunatic! It was raw and real. It was about passion and pride. It meant so much to him. It is an unbelievable memory that will stay with me forever.'

Although Leitrim were to lose the All-Ireland semi-final Darcy was literally to leave his mark.

'As captain when I shook hands with John O'Leary as the photo shows I was so fired up I nearly squashed John's hand. He told me afterwards that I nearly broke two or three of his fingers and that he thought I had done it deliberately but it was just because I was pumped up.

'It was a fantastic achievement for the team and when I led them out onto Croke Park and although it meant a lot to the county I was really thinking about all those training sessions we had suffered in Strand Hill. This was the reward for the sacrifices, the endless travel to training sessions and the blood, sweat and tears.

'For Leitrim people just to be in Croke Park one day in their lives was such a proud moment for them. That's the magic of the GAA. It is so much more than football.

'We didn't do ourselves justice in the semi-final and the next year we left the game against Galway behind us in the Connacht championship. If we had won I believe we would have retained the Connacht final and given a much better showing in the All-Ireland semi-final. I know Armagh's Enda McNulty and he often says that they should have won more than one All-Ireland. I tell him that they were lucky to win one because it is so hard to make a breakthrough when you have no tradition of winning.'

When John O'Mahony stepped down as Leitrim manager in 1996 it was obvious that things were on a downward spiral. What was it about O'Mahony that made him achieve success with Leitrim?

'One thing is his man management and the belief that he gives you. He was very good at talking to players. In 1994 he told me that he didn't want to see me in a chipper, not that I was into that anyway. After we won the Connacht final he told me he didn't want to see me drinking because I was the public face of the team and had to project the right image for the lads.

'I remember a very tight game against Galway in Carrick-on-Shannon and we got a potentially decisive free about forty yards out. Two or three of our lads ran over to take it but John came running to the sideline and roared at the top of his voice: "Dec, I want you to take it." He believed in me to score this vital kick and because he believed in me I had confidence that I would. To an outsider it looked a pressure kick but I felt totally calm because of what Johnno had said. It was very emotional when John left – both for us and for Johnno.'

Although Leitrim were not to reach those dizzy heights again they did find themselves in the headlines once more.

'We were playing Mayo on a live game for RTÉ and a mêlée broke out and the Mayo manager John Maughan came running onto the pitch in his shorts. He passed a comment to Gerry Flanagan and Gerry floored him. In our view Maughan definitely deserved it but it's probably not the thing to do on live TV! Pat Spillane and the pundits were outraged but it did Flanagan's reputation no harm in Leitrim!'

Some of the same fans who were throwing bouquets at Darcy in 1994 were swinging cleavers when he decided to transfer to Dublin though many of his friends and Leitrim fans wished him well.

'Once the offer was made, I had to give it serious thought. At the time the '94 Leitrim side were disintegrating. The changes weren't to my liking. One little incident encapsulated it for me. The day before we played a Connacht championship match we were having lunch and were given steaks. In pretty much his last Championship game Mickcy Quinn said he wouldn't eat steak, he would only eat chicken because it was the best meal for the match the next day. Here was this Leitrim legend on his last legs worrying about his diet but when I went out of the hotel I saw two of the new players, very talented guys, smoking. That was their way of preparing for the biggest game of their lives. To be honest, if Mickey was going to continue playing, I wouldn't have been able to walk away from Leitrim because I looked up to him so much and so admired his great commitment to the county.

'The hardest thing for me was leaving Aughawillian. I had played in seven county finals, two Connacht finals and won a three-in-a-row with them. Some of the people there were like a second family to me. The easy thing for me to have done would have been to stay in Leitrim where I would always be a hero because of '94. I wanted to win an All-Ireland not a popularity contest. Part of me had always been curious about whether I would have been good enough to win my place on the Dublin side, particularly when they won the All-Ireland in 1995. I remember meeting Paul Bealin and he said to me: "I'll give you balls for doing it alone." I wanted to test myself and if I failed at least I had given it a go.'

Darcy is no Edith Piaf. He has some regrets about his time with Dublin.

'I had a good first year or two with Dublin but I made a big mistake when I came into the dressing room first and didn't say to players like Keith Barr: "Get the finger out of your arse and start playing." They were all experienced and gifted players and part of me thought who was I to be telling them what to do. I should have let loose but Dublin is a closed shop and I wanted to make friends. Mickey Whelan was the trainer in my first year and I felt his training was very advanced but it needed the players to take some of the responsibility themselves but they were letting him down. I felt I was a newcomer and held my tongue. Towards the end I did say what I felt I ought be done but I should have done that so much earlier.

'In '95 I picked up a back injury in my Leitrim days. We were due to play Dublin in Croke Park in the League and there was no way I was going to miss out on that. After the match, though, I was in agony and needed surgery. My surgeon Stephen Young told me: "You'll never play football to the level you played before again." I said: "You are having a laugh. I'll defy you." I was only twenty-five but looking back, it was the start of a whole series of injuries that stopped me from putting together a run of top performances.

'We came very close in 2002 when Ray Cosgrave almost equalised against Armagh but to be honest, I believe Tommy Carr had a better team. John Bailey, then the county chairman, told us after the drawn game against Kerry in the All-Ireland quarter final in 2001 that no matter what happened Tommy Carr would be staying for the next year. He actually cried with emotion as he said that but less than a month later he put the knife into Tommy. Players would have done anything for Tommy but we didn't do enough for him. I felt sorry for him because he was very unlucky, none more so than with the Maurice Fitzgerald sideline that drew the match for Kerry the first day. Tommy was as honest as the day was long and was fiercely driven. There was nothing he wouldn't have done for Dublin. He was probably a better manager at the end but had more to learn and I think it's a shame he didn't get the chance.

'I have ever experienced anything like Thurles those two days. I had heard about Munster finals but was not prepared for the atmosphere in the square. It was amazing and packed with people. I remember hearing the sirens as the Kerry team were arriving and it was like the Germans were coming.'

The Thurles experience did provide Darcy with the most amusing incident in his career.

'We were staying in the Horse and Jockey and I went out for a walk with one of the lads. A car pulled in beside us and my colleague said, "There's your man."

"Who?"

"Your man from Star Trek."

It was Colm Meaney and he was walking into the car park. The next thing I knew I heard a booming voice shouting: "Hey Colm. Beam me up Scottie." It was Vinny Murphy standing at the window. He was as naked as the day he was born!

'Vinny was a character. He loved a fag. Some wag changed the sign in Parnell Park from: "No Smoking" to "No Smoking Vinny!"

Darcy continues to be involved in the game through coaching St Brigids, a side managed by Gerry McEntee, a tough, uncompromising star of the Meath team of the 1980s. 'Gerry manages the way he played!'

With Jim Gavin, Darcy coached the Dublin Under-21 side to an All-Ireland in 2003, though the team was officially managed by Tommy Lyons. What was their relationship with Lyons at the time?

'It was frosty enough. If Tommy walked into this room now I would have great craic with him but I don't agree with his approach to management. To me management is all about the team. It's not about courting popularity with the media or putting yourself or your profile ahead of the team. He had a very different agenda to Tommy Carr.'

Many of that Under-21 team have graduated into the senior ranks. Who were the players Darcy knew would make it?

'Alan Brogan was always going to be a great player. Bryan Cullen stood out as a player and a leader. He had that serious drive and determination that you need to be a winner. We had a celebration after we won the Leinster title and after it all the boys went to pubs or night clubs except Bryan. When I asked him why he said: "I've won nothing yet. I want to win an All-Ireland".'

Although he failed to win an All-Ireland medal, the glass is half full for Darcy.

'The greatest achievement for me now is when I meet guys like Peter Canavan or Kieran McGeeney and they say: "Howya Declan?" To have that kind of respect means a lot. It is much more important to me than any medal.' Darcy's dream team is:

1. John O'Leary
(Dublin)

2. Seán Óg de Paor     3. Darren Fay     4. Tony Scullion
(Galway)     (Meath)     (Derry)

5. Paul Curran     6. Kieran McGeeney     7. Seamus Moynihan
(Dublin)     (Armagh)     (Kerry)

8. Darragh Ó Sé     9. Jack O'Shea
(Kerry)     (Kerry)

10. Peter Canavan     11. Greg Blaney     12. Maurice Fitzgerald
(Tyrone)     (Down)     (Kerry)

13. Mickey Linden     14. Kevin O'Brien     15. Tony McManus
(Down)     (Wicklow)     (Roscommon)

Teak Tough Defenders

# The Lynch Mob

## Brendan Lynch

It was Jimmy Murray who catapulted Brendan Lynch, one of four Roscommon players to be selected on the Connacht team of the Millennium, into national prominence.

'I was playing a senior club match for Oran in 1941 and this man approached me and asked me if I was a minor. I thought he was asking me if I worked as a miner because in my innocence at the time I didn't know what minor meant as a football term. I told him I wasn't but that I was in the reserves. He was a bit frustrated by my response but explained that Roscommon were playing Mayo in the Connacht minor final and if they won I could be playing in the All-Ireland semi-final a week later in Tralee. At the time travelling to Tralee was as unimaginable to me as travelling to the Antarctic today. I asked him who he was and he told me he was Jimmy Murray from Knockcroghery. That night I listened to the news on the battery set radio which was the only programme we were allowed to listen to because of the Emergency but I kept it on to hear Sean Ó Ceallacháin reading the sports news. I heard that Roscommon had won. The problem was I didn't know then if I would play or not. I went back to The Curragh and when I heard nothing by Friday lunch-time I was despondent. Then later that afternoon I was on duty when I was relieved at my post and told I had to get the train home to Roscommon and join up with the team. The problem was that I had very little time to get to the station. The hackney car wasn't there so I started to run the few miles to the station. With ten minutes left I stopped running because I knew I couldn't make it. Then I saw a private coming on his bicycle in the opposite direction. I was a corporal so I had one stripe and he had none so I told him to give me the bike and I left it at the station for him.

'We sneaked a draw in Austin Stack Park and beat them easily in a

*Preceding page:* Thanks a bunch: Brendan Lynch (second from left) hovers as Roscommon clear the defence in the 1943 All-Ireland final. *Photo:* Tony Conboy

replay. Then we beat Louth in the final. I had played three matches and won an All-Ireland medal.'

A human history book and eighty-five years young, Lynch's mind is as sharp as an executioner's axe. Over sixty years on from his inter-county debut, he is amused by the amateur nature of Roscommon football which saw him left on the subs' bench in favour of an established player with a big name in the county who was over the hill for the 1942 Connacht Championship. In 1943, though, Lynch had established the right-half-back position as his own and announced his arrival on the national stage in the All-Ireland semi-final against Louth.

'I was marking Peter Corr who had been the player of the year at that stage. He had scored thirteen points in the Leinster final. I decided it was his career or mine. I handled him roughly and kept him scoreless. Peter, who was related to the singers the Corrs, went on to play for Everton.

'My lasting memory from the game was when County Secretary John Joe Fahy came running up to me at the end of the game and said: "Ye'll beat them in the second half if you play like that." I turned to him and said: "We have already." He looked shocked and said: "God, did I miss it?" He was so embroiled in the whole game and the tension it created he had lost all track of time.

'I remember seeing Tom Shevlin playing when I was a boy. He was Roscommon's greatest player in the 1920s. I met him as I came out of Croke Park. He said to me: "Ye were lucky." I said: "We won." He laughed and replied: "That's the end of the argument."

'We beat Cavan in the All-Ireland final after a replay. I marked Mick Higgins who was very quiet and a very clean and good footballer. What I remember most was the mayhem at the end. First Cavan's Joe Stafford was sent off after having a go at Owensie Hoare. We got a point but Barney Culley didn't agree and put the umpire into the net with a box. Big Tom O'Reilly, the captain of Cavan, came into remonstrate and T. P. O'Reilly threw the referee in the air.'

It was not the medal that mattered to Lynch.

'The euphoria of winning was incredible. I felt like jumping out of my skin. I was on top of the world. I was twenty years of age and the world seemed my oyster. I've given away all my medals to my family. I read that Christy Ring had donated one of his All-Ireland medals to the foreign missions and I did the same. It was the sense of achievement that mattered most to me.'

Roscommon had a slice of luck before claiming a second title in 1944. 'Sligo drew with us in the first round of the Connacht Championship

*Above (left):* Crimecall: Brendan Lynch in his professional attire during his time stationed in Kerry in the 1950s; (right): The Lynch-pin: Brendan Lynch takes a trip down memory lane as he makes a speech at the Westmanstown Sports Centre in 2003, sixty years after winning his first All-Ireland title.

in Boyle. They should have beaten us. We were lucky to survive. There were only two-thousand people in attendance when we played Mayo in the Connacht final because of the transport problems during the War. We were worried by Cavan at half-time in the All-Ireland semi-final but they collapsed completely in the second half and we had an easy win. The belief then was that you hadn't really won an All-Ireland until you beat Kerry in a final so we were all keen to do that. I was marking the famous Paddy Bawn Brosnan. He was a fisherman and fond of the women, fond of the porter and fond of the rough and tumble!

'I made the most impact on their great midfielder Paddy Kennedy when I had a head collision with him and he had to be stretchered off. He asked me: "Jaysus, what did you do to me?"'

Roscommon were not to recapture the same winning feeling again. 'We were unlucky with illness. Phelim Murray got TB and spent twelve months in a sanatorium. I would consider Phelim to be Roscommon's best ever footballer. The nearest to him I have seen since was Dermot Earley who was close to perfect. TB also finished Liam Gilmartin's career. We also lost John Joe Nerney so we were never the same force again.

'Mayo beat us in the first round of the Championship in 1945. We were suffering from burnout and they were hungry. It was a relief in a way because you had the chance to take holidays. I met Jimmy Murray that summer and he asked me how I was finding the summer without football. When I said I thought it was great he told me he felt the same.'

Roscommon were to come within a whisker of taking another All-Ireland in 1946.

'It was a Mickey Mouse ruling in the GAA that cost us the title. We played Mayo in the Connacht final in Ballinasloe. They had a goal disallowed and then we got a goal that was going to be disallowed. Jimmy Murray grabbed the green flag and waved it and we were awarded the goal. After the game Mayo lodged an objection. What should have happened was that the referee should have produced his report saying Roscommon won the match and that would have been that. Instead we had to go into a replay and on top of the heavy collective training we were doing we didn't need another match. We lost Frank Kinlough with a leaky valve in his heart and Doc Callaghan, our full-back, was injured. By the time we faced Kerry in the All-Ireland final replay, they were getting stronger and we were getting weaker. I was never as happy as when the final whistle sounded in that game because the whole year had been absolutely exhausting with the two replays and all the collective training. To quote Shakespeare: "If all the year were a playing holiday, To sport would be as tedious as to work."

'It finished us a team. We lost to Cavan in the All-Ireland semi-final in '47, which meant they went on to play in the Polo Grounds instead of us. I didn't begrude them. It was only right that players like John Joe O'Reilly finally won an All-Ireland.'

As Roscommon's fortunes faded Lynch found himself, in a fit of desperation by the selectors, playing at full-forward. From his point of view the initial experiment worked disastrously well as he scored two goals and was kept in the purgatory of the full-forward position for longer than he wished.

'I found out that full-backs are really kicking jennets. A full-forward needs to be an animal. Our great midfielder Eamon Boland might have survived up there. I always thought he had four elbows and four joints.'

Injury meant that Lynch's career ended prematurely after another Connacht title victory in 1952. His work as a Garda Superintendent continued to bring him into contact with some famous GAA figures.

'When I moved to Tralee I got to know Dan Spring, father of

Dick and an All-Ireland wininng captain in 1940 himself, very well. He would contact me before court day to let me know he "had an interest" in a particular case. Once the verdict was in he would be back to me and generally the penalty was light, like a small fine, so he just wanted to be the first to tell the family the good news. There was a local Fianna Fáil TD for the area who tried to influence one of my colleagues in a particular case. When my associate refused to play ball with him he unsuccessfully tried to intimidate him by implying he would have him transferred but he never tried that tactic on me.

'In my first week I found myself prosecuting a man for a drunk-driving charge. He called a number of character witnesses. The first was six-foot-four, was wearing no shirt but instead Wellingtons and an overcoat. I thought to myself: "What sort of an Arab is this?" I then checked his name. It was Con Houlihan. In his cross-examination he was asked: "Do you take a drink yourself?"

"In a social capacity?"

"How much would you drink?"

"Not too much . . . Ten or twelve pints at the one sitting."

'The next time I met him was in O'Connell Street. He was wearing runners. I wouldn't mind if it was a pair but he was wearing two odd ones!'

Lynch's dream team from the men of his era is:

1. Tim Burke
(Mayo)

| 2. J.P. (Tot) McGaughan | 3. Eddie Boyle | 4. Tadhg Healy |
|---|---|---|
| (Mayo) | (Louth) | (Kerry) |

| 5. Peter O'Reilly | 6. Bill Carlos | 7. Phelim Murray |
|---|---|---|
| (Dublin) | (Roscommon) | (Roscommon) |

| 8. Eamon Boland | 9. Paddy Kennedy |
|---|---|
| (Roscommon) | (Kerry) |

| 10. Mick Higgins | 11. Tony Tighe | 12. Paddy Bawn Brosnan |
|---|---|---|
| (Cavan) | (Cavan) | (Kerry) |

| 13. Josie Mulleney | 14. Tom Langan | 15. Mick Flanagan |
|---|---|---|
| (Mayo) | (Mayo) | (Mayo) |

# Paddy's Days

## Paddy Prendergast

Throughout his long life Paddy Prendergast has always been given interesting advice. As a teenager his Latin and Irish teacher told him: 'Treat women like Kerry men do. Get them young, treat them rough and tell them nothing.' However, it was advice from a man destined to become a very close friend that had the most impact on his football career. The Ballintubber native, an authority on the history of Ballintubber Abbey from its opening in 1216 to its flouting of the Penal Laws by remaining open, had just endured one of the most difficult days of his career.

'In 1947 I made my debut for Mayo. I was stationed in Dungloe with the guards at the time and had played with Donegal for a year or so at that stage when the invitation came to play for Mayo. I had a severe dilemma because I was very happy where I was and I knew very few fellas on the Mayo team. On the day of the match I travelled down to Ballina for a challenge match against Galway, via bus and taxi, but typical of the County Board they didn't think of getting me a few shillings to cover my travel expenses. I was brought around and introduced to the players before the game.

'I was selected at full-back but at that stage I was a midfielder. On my right was John Forde, on my left was Seán Flanagan. I was marking Ned Keogh. The first ball that came in Ned sold me a dummy and scored a goal with his right. The next ball he sidestepped me and scored a goal with his left. Seán Flanagan shouted at me: "What in the name of Christ are you doing there?" With the small bit of dignity I could muster I replied: "To be frank, I have no idea."

'After the match Seán took me aside and somehow produced a foolscap page and gave me a tutorial into the basics of full-back play. It was like a class of advanced trigonometry but it was the beginning of a very strong and lasting friendship.'

It was also the start of a glorious adventure for Mayo football.

'Nobody expected us to go anywhere. Quite frankly, neither did I. We got together for collective training in Mrs Gaughan's guesthouse in Ballina before the 1948 Championship. We were under the watchful eyes of Gerald Courell and Jackie Carney who welded us into a team. They were very disciplined and there was no drinking nor womanising tolerated. It was the making of us as a team. Living together and sharing breakfast every morning bonded us together. At night a blackboard was produced and every aspect of the game offensively as well as defensively was gone into as well as the strengths and weaknesses of the opposition. We were not the typical team for the time. We only had one farmer, but he was a big farmer, Henry Dixon. We had four or five lawyers, about as many doctors, an engineer, and a priest. Peter Quinn was newly ordained at the time and the lads exaggerated their atheistic elements just to wind him up. They were intelligent fellas who believed in themselves.

'While we won two All-Irelands I believe we should have won a four-in-a row from 1948 to '51. We tailed Cavan by a point but were playing with a gale in the 1948 All-Ireland final with three and a half minutes to go when the referee blew for full-time. I am certain we would have beaten them if we had played the full match. There was no objection but it was savage really that this should have happened.

'In 1949 the belief was that we would win the All-Ireland semi-final by ten points. After twenty-four minutes Seán Flanagan and I had a chat about how much we were going to win by. Then, inexplicably, the county selectors took off two of our half-backs and replaced them with two forwards. The Meath half-forwards started to waltz through them. The

*Below:* The generation gap: Paddy Prendergast relaxes with his grandson Will in the family back garden in 2007.

incompetence of the County Board knew no bounds. Their madness cost us an All-Ireland that year. If it was today we wouldn't have accepted it.'

The ineptitude of the selectors almost cost Mayo the All-Ireland in 1950. 'We had probably the best goalkeeper in the country at the time in Seán Wynne and he was in excellent form for us all year. Then for some crazy reason he was dropped for the All-Ireland final against Louth and Billy Durkin was brought in for him. Understandably Billy was very nervous and the first ball he handled he dropped it. Seán Flanagan knew we were in trouble and pulled Billy aside. He signalled to the sideline that Billy was injured and Wynne came in for him. Only for Seán doing that we would have probably lost that All-Ireland.

'I remember the joy was unconfined after the game. People don't realise how different Ireland was back then. We were on our knees in economic terms. The GAA made an awful difference to people at such a black time. The bonfires that blazed after we won were a sign that people could still have hope.'

Another All-Ireland came in '51 but legend has it that it was then that the seeds of Mayo's woes were sown for decades to come.

'People tell it slightly differently but the core story is that when we returned with the Sam Maguire Cup in 1951 we interrupted either a Mass or a funeral and the priest was so enraged that he put a curse on the team that we would never win the All-Ireland again while any of that team were on earth.'

Prendergast was to have one more opportunity for glory in 1955.

'We had a great chance of beating Dublin and qualifying for another All-Ireland final. We were lodged in their half throughout the second half but still we couldn't put them away. It was to become an all too familiar story for Mayo for decades to come.

'Since I retired I look at the failures of Mayo as my personal via dolorosa. At the moment I hardly want to see them play. It pains me to see them lose games they should have won like the All-Ireland against Meath in '96. I am tired looking at their failures and their lack of determination. You won't win All-Irelands unless you have courage and determination.'

One aspect of modern football really grates on him. 'I hate the cult of the manager. A good manager will bring organisation but it is fifteen good players that win All-Irelands. The financial end troubles me also. Two questions I want to ask about these managers: how much are these managers getting paid?; are they worth it?'

Prendergast's work as a garda brought him to Kerry where he formed a close friendship with one of the icons of Kerry football.

'Paddy Bawn Brosnan was a lovely human being and at that stage had a pub in Dingle. He had a great feeling for Mayo and I spent a lot of time with him. One time Seán Flanagan came down to visit me I brought him to see the Bawn. We went into a quiet nook of the pub and chatted for hours. What I most remember about it though was over the course of the evening thirty people must have peered into the nook just to get a glimpse of Paddy Bawn, such was his legendary status. It was like going to Lourdes. Kerry had such wonderful players. I always felt that Paddy Kennedy was the prince of footballers. He was majestic.'

Most of the Mayo team of '50 and '51 have passed on. It is like a litany of sadness as Prendergast goes through all the funerals.

'The first to go was Mick Flanagan from cancer. He was the closest friend I had on the team. He died at a very young age. He was the most wonderful human being. He would give you his heart and anything else you needed.'

The happy memories remain. 'We had great characters in the team. John Forde was very serious. When we stayed in Mrs Gaughan's guesthouse our routine was to go for a ten-mile walk after breakfast. Before a big game against Kerry Tom Langan said he was going to skip the walk that day because his stomach wasn't too good. Then Mick Flanagan said he would not go either because his leg wasn't too good. John jumped up and said: "For Jaysus' sake, wire Kerry and award them the game!"'

One of Prendergast's big admirers was the late Mick Dunne. This was reflected when I invited Dunne to select his dream team:

1. Johnny Geraghty
(Galway)

2. Enda Colleran     3. Paddy Prendergast    4. Seán Flanagan
(Galway)          (Mayo)           (Meath)

5. Jerome O'Shea    6. Gerry O'Malley    7. Martin O'Connell
(Kerry)          (Roscommon)         (Meath)

8. Mick O'Connell        9. Jack O'Shea
(Kerry)                (Kerry)

10. Seán O'Neill    11. Seán Purcell    12. Micheál Kearins
(Down)           (Galway)          (Sligo)

13. Packy McGarty    14. Kevin Heffernan    15. John Egan
(Leitrim)          (Dublin)          (Kerry)

# No Johnny Come Lately

## Johnny Hughes

Born into a family of fourteen, Johnny Hughes made his senior debut for Galway in 1959.

'I was only nineteen and one weekday evening, I went down to play a challenge match against Tipperary. It was really a case of Galway being short of players but it was a real baptism of fire. Those Tipperary lads were very tough! It was two years before I played for the seniors again, in Wembley against Derry.'

An injury delayed his opportunity to stake a claim for a regular place on the team. He was a sub on the side that lost the Connacht semi-final to Roscommon in 1972 but was a regular on the Galway team that marched triumphantly through the Connacht championship the following year. Expectations across the county side were heightened as Galway accounted for an Offaly side seeking three All-Irelands in a row but their hopes were dashed – not for the first or last time.

'I was in my prime and my lifetime's ambition to play in an All-Ireland had been realised. We had a blow going into the match when we lost our star forward Johnny Tobin. Nineteen-year-old Morgan Hughes came in for him. He had the onerous responsibility of taking the frees but he handled the pressure very well. We scored 2-13 and lost the All-Ireland by seven points. Jimmy Barry Murphy and Jimmy Barrett caused us untold trouble. I have no cribs about losing in 1973 because we were comprehensively beaten. We couldn't match their firepower.

'I wasn't too downbeat after that. I felt we had a good team and had the ability to win two or three All-Irelands later. One of the strange things about it all was although John Dunne was our trainer we had the crazy situation of having twelve or fourteen selectors. You could have made a team out of them.'

There was an entertaining epilogue to Galway's lost All-Ireland.

'After the All-Ireland we were staying in the Grand Hotel but our function was in another hotel. A few of us, like "Boxcar Willie", which

was our nickname for Billy Joyce because he always led the singing and had more success with women than the rest of us, wanted some female company. We had a very strict porter in our hotel and there was no way he was letting any of us bring girls up to our rooms. We discovered a bit of timber down the basement and we got the women in by getting them to walk the plank and by pushing them in through the windows.'

In 1974 Galway were back in the All-Ireland final against Dublin having easily saw off Donegal in the semi-final.

'Johnny Tobin had an outstanding game in the semi-final, scoring almost at will. You are better off though if you have a set of forwards who can score two or three points each rather than being over dependent on one player. If he is tied down you are in big trouble as we discovered in the '74 final when Johnny was held to a point. I vividly remember we had at least seventy-five per cent of the possession but again it came back to the same old story: lack of firepower up front. I got my second point with nine minutes to go to tie the match but Jimmy Keaveney got a point from the kickout and then another one and they beat us by five points in the end.'

The key incident in the match was when Liam Sammon, who had

*Left:* And so this is Christmas: Johnny Hughes displays his two All-Star awards, won in 1974 and 1976.

*Facing page:* Go Johnny Go: Johnny Hughes (on extreme left) awaits the breaking ball as Roscommon plays Galway.
*Photo:* Tony Conboy

never missed a penalty for Galway before the final, had his spot-kick saved by Paddy Cullen.

'I don't regard Liam's penalty as our worst miss although if it had gone in we'd probably have won. In that game we had forwards who were kicking the ball straight at Paddy Cullen when he was lying on the ground. Throughout the match we missed chances that were easier to score. I was very disappointed that we lost that game. I was still young and never imagined that I would have to wait another nine years to play in an All-Ireland.'

Some consolation for Hughes came when his club Mountbellew won the Galway County Championship that year. This meant that he would captain his county the following year. Things did not go to plan, though, in the Connacht championship.

'I was really looking forward to the campaign in 1975 because I was captain. At that stage there was a lot of concern in Galway about our forwards. Pat Donnellan was playing well at club level and was drafted in late on for our first Championship match against Sligo. He wasn't originally in our first twenty-two and was wearing the number twenty-four jersey. I still recall the comment in the paper the next day: "Pat Donnellan appeared on the scene wearing a faded jersey and the jersey, no more than the man, belonged to another decade." Micheál Kearins beat us on his own that day. Anything he got inside the fifty-yard line went over the bar. He was like radar. On a personal level it was very disappointing to go out so early.'

The Nestor Cup was back in Galway in 1976 but Dublin beat them narrowly in the All-Ireland semi-final. It was a game Galway could have won. The rest of the seventies was a bleak decade for Galway as Roscommon won four consecutive Connacht titles. In 1981, Galway were back in the big time again, beating Roscommon to win the National League final despite playing much of the match with only fourteen men after Stephen Joyce was sent off. It was a win against the odds in more ways than one.

'Around this time we had a bit of problem with our management. Liam O'Neill was put in charge of us and he wanted to pick his own two or three selectors which would have been the sensible thing to. Common sense did not prevail but Liam stuck to his guns and on principle stood down. Mattie McDonagh took over and brought us to victory in the League final.'

Yet again, Galway snatched defeat from the jaws of victory in the Connacht championship against Mayo. A serious injury in a club match consigned Hughes to the sidelines for a year. He returned to the fold when coming on as a substitute against Offaly in the All-Ireland semi-final.

'I was thirty-one when I had my injury. I had a bone taken from under my knee and a plate and five screws inserted. A lot of people had thought I would never come back. That semi-final was not a game we could have won; it is a game we should have won. It was the story of my footballing life. We lost by a point having missed so many frees it was untrue. What was worse was that Offaly went on to stop Kerry from winning the five-in-a-row.'

If he thought 1982 was disappointing, it paled into insignificance when compared with the disaster that lay around the corner in 1983.

'That year I had come back from a serious injury and got myself into the best shape of my life. I was absolutely flying at that stage. In the All-Ireland semi-final against Donegal, I remember turning quick for the ball and getting a twinge in the groin. I felt sore immediately after the match. The next morning I couldn't get out of bed. I trained very little before the All-Ireland but I kept the scale of my injury a dark secret from the media and from Mattie McDonagh. The morning of the All-Ireland I walked to Mass from the hotel. I was walking on the edge of the footpath when my foot slipped over the edge. It was like a knife had been stuck in my leg and torn away the side. I went back to the hotel after Mass and as I lay on my bed I said to myself, "You fool. Don't you dare go out and play in this match."

'On the other hand, this voice was saying in my head, "You've been playing for thirteen years and this is Galway's year. We're going to win the All-Ireland." I let the heart rule the head and I decided to play.

'The game wasn't long on before I could feel the leg going. Because of the injury, I was unable to make a quick turn and had to turn in a semi-circle. At one stage I made a foray up the field and as I went to kick the ball, it was like someone cut a lump out of my leg. I had to go off with about fifteen or twenty minutes to go.

'Early in the game we were playing well against the wind. I could see that the Dublin forwards were a bit worried. I remember telling our goalkeeper, Padraig Coyne, to take his time with the kickouts. If he could waste two or three minutes in the first half for us against the wind then all the better for us. It was inexperience on Padraig's part that he took the infamous quick kick out which fell short to Barney Rock and he lobbed the ball into our net. We were struggling and it was certainly backs to the wall after that but we were still in the game. We had so many chances. You'd nearly have to compliment our forwards. They were kicking spectacular wides when it seemed much, much easier to score!

'I have agonised about my decision to play in that game throughout the years. I've often thought that if I hadn't started in that game and came on for the last twenty minutes, maybe in the forwards, we might have won that game. I would at least have been able to punch the ball over the bar.

'It was the closest I ever got to seeing a dressing room turn into a morgue. I was sick, sore and sorry: really, really sore and sorry. It was my last game for Galway and was a nightmare way to finish. Had I not played in the final I might have been able to play again for Galway the following year; that's if I would have wanted to have played for another year. As it was at one stage it was felt that I might never walk properly again. It was two and a half years before I played football again and I had the pleasure of finishing my career by winning another county title with Mountbellew. Some people only get one chance to win an All-Ireland. We got three and blew them all but that last one was just such a heartbreak.'

The game was overshadowed by a series of ugly incidents which led to three players from Dublin being sent off and one from Galway. Why did the game turn so nasty?

'I remember a fairly hefty challenge from one of our players on one of the Dublin lads. Tomás Tierney was sent off but it should have been that other player. Tomás was playing very well and it was a big blow for us. Kieran Duff was sent off for apparently kicking one of our lads on the ground but I think that incident looked much worse than it was. There was no real contact made.'

What, then, about the infamous tunnel incident said to have involved Brian Mullins and Brian Talty at the interval?

'In those situations players get very hyped up and things that normally wouldn't happen unfortunately do. Having said that, I honestly don't know what happened. I didn't see anything. I never asked anyone what happened because I never wanted to know. From the moment the final whistle went and for the last twenty-five years I have done everything I can to forget everything about that game. It's the one match of my career I've hardly ever spoken to anyone about until now. It's the only one of my All-Ireland final appearances I have on video but I've never watched it and I can never see me putting myself through that nightmare again. I really have no interest in finding out who did what in the tunnel. All I will say is that whatever happened in the tunnel should not have been brought onto the field in the second half.'

There are happier memories from his time with Galway for Hughes to reflect on.

'When we were training in Tuam, there would always be fellas looking for shampoo afterwards. I always had shampoo but Tomás Tierney and Tommy Joe Gilmore were always swiping some off me. I was working for a chemical company and we manufactured a light oil which looked like clinic shampoo. I poured some of it into an empty bottle of shampoo which I left outside my shower in the dressing room. I hid a bottle of shampoo in my bag and I went in to the shower with some of it in my hand. A few seconds later I saw Tierney's foot coming over and taking the bottle of shampoo but I didn't let on to see him. He rubbed it into his hair and passed it on to Tommy Joe. A few minutes later all hell broke loose. I can tell you it stopped them from stealing my shampoo for a long time after that.'

He is a warm, affable man and the most revealing insight into Johnny's personality is that the only photo of his career evident in his home is almost completely hidden by the stereo. This impression is confirmed when the trophies that are most prominently displayed are not his two All-Star awards (1974 and 1976 at wing-back) nor his two awards for Galway Footballer of the Year (1974 and 1980) but those of his three daughters for athletics and camogie.

Who was the greatest character he came across?

'Frank McGuigan was my most difficult opponent. He was both very strong and very skilful and could take you to the cleaners and he had two great feet and a great head. He was also the best character I ever came across. We went on an All-Stars trip together. I was the captain of the team and Frank had been out on the town all night. I remember knocking on his door and wondering would he be able to get up knowing he had only an hour and a half's sleep. He got up and destroyed Brian Mullins in the Dublin midfield and was head and shoulders above any other player on the day. Frank took it upon himself to organise the social side of things and he took us to the sort of places some of us had never been in before!'

When his inter-county career finished, Hughes found a new outlet for his skills through his involvement in charity matches with the Jimmy Magee All-Stars.

'Jimmy is a great character. I really enjoyed playing in those All-Star games with him. I always did a running commentary on those matches as I was playing in them much to Jimmy's delight.

'One day before one match Jimmy was giving the team-talk to boost our morale. He put his hand on our wing-back Fr Brian D'Arcy's shoulder and said, "Brian. In years to come GAA people will be sitting around their fires and they'll be talking about the great wing-backs of all time," and he paused and you could see Brian's chest swelling with pride, "and you know something Brian, when they do: you won't even get a mention!"'

Johnny decided to chose a dream team of players, like himself, who had never won an All-Ireland medal from his own era. However, he decided to exclude Galway players.

1. Brian McAlinden
(Armagh)

2. Harry Keegan     3. Gerry McCarville     4. Gabriel Kelly
(Roscommon)     (Monaghan)     (Cavan)

5. Ger Feeney     6. Paddy Moriarty     7. Danny Murray
(Mayo)     (Armagh)     (Roscommon)

8. Willie Joe Padden     9. Dermot Earley
(Mayo)     (Roscommon)

10. Peter McGinnity     11. Frank McGuigan     12. Micheál Kearins
(Fermanagh)     (Tyrone)     (Sligo)

13. Tony McManus     14. Eugene McKenna     15. Nudie Hughes
(Roscommon)     (Tyrone)     (Monaghan)

# An Officer and a Gentleman

## Pat Lindsay

*Above:* Pat on the Back: Pat Lindsay holds the League cup aloft after captaining Roscommon to its only League triumph in 1979 when they defeated Cork.

The early 1970s were formative years for Roscommon's finest full-back Pat Lindsay. In 1971 he made his senior debut for Roscommon in a defeat to Kerry in a league game in Tralee and the following year he made a major career choice.

'I saw a job advertised for a prison officer and I applied for it. I was twenty-two, got no training and on the first day I found myself on duty in Mountjoy. Although I didn't get a third level education, my education in life was from the prison service. I learned a lot from my colleagues and I learned a lot from prisoners.'

1972 was also a milestone on the football front.

'We beat Mayo in the Connacht final with a very young side. Our oldest player was Jimmy Finnegan who was twenty-six. We were badly beaten by Kerry in the All-Ireland semi-final. The big disappointment was not that we lost but that we didn't play as well as we could. The same thing happened against Kerry in the semi-final in 1978. Losing but playing well may not be much of a consolation but it is a consolation. When you get to Croke Park and play one of the top teams, you want to play to your best and it hurts when you fail to do so. I should say I always looked forward to playing Kerry. They are the aristocrats of football. They are the yardstick to measure how good you are, personally and as a team.'

Two years later Kerry ruined Roscommon's hopes again.

'We completely outplayed them in every sector of the field in the National League final but John Egan got a last minute goal to equalise the game. They beat us easily in the replay. To beat Kerry in a national final in Croke Park would have been a huge boost to that team and set us up for greater things. Instead we were again badly beaten in the Connacht final by a very strong Galway side who were unlucky not to have won an All-Ireland final in the early 1970s.'

Although 1977 saw Lindsay rewarded on a personal level with an All-Star award, it was another year of might-have-beens for Roscommon.

'We were seven points up with ten minutes to go in the All-Ireland semi-final against Armagh but we lost concentration and let them back to draw the game. You could feel the giddiness running through the team. We thought we had one foot in the All-Ireland final. We were shellshocked in the dressing room afterwards. We had been much better than them but in the replay they beat us by a point.

'It was pretty much the same story two years later when we snatched defeat from the jaws of victory against Dublin in the semi-final. If we had won either of those two semi-finals the experience of having played an All-Ireland final would have been invaluable when we took on

Kerry in the 1980 final.'

Again there were some crumbs of comfort for Lindsay in 1979 when he captained Roscommon to its first and only National League title, with a crushing defeat of a star-laden Cork team. His Roscommon colleagues would not allow him to get too big for his boots though: 'Eamon McManus said to me: "If you ever get up the midfield area that's for skilful players, pass the ball to someone with a bit of skill!"'

Roscommon had won the All-Ireland Under-21 final in 1978 and had picked up some really class players from that side; Tony McManus, Seamus Hayden, Mick Finneran and Gerry Connellan.

'The spine of the team were very experienced but the new lads brought another dimension. Tom Heneghan had come in as our manager. He was ahead of his time as a coach. With Tony, Mick and John O'Connor in our forward line we had three guys who could get you scores. Their worth was really shown in the All-Ireland semi-final in 1980 against Armagh when, after failing in four previous semi-finals, we finally qualified for the All-Ireland. Tony Mc's goal that day typified what our forward line was capable of. Tom once said to us: "Our tactics are very simple; get the ball fast into the forwards." There was none of the passing to the side or even backwards that you see today.

'It was just incredible to reach the All-Ireland final in 1980. Tom had us really well prepared. He arranged for us to get two weeks off work and for those two weeks we trained twice a day, at noon and in the early evening. By night time you couldn't wait to get to bed. We had Kerry reeling

*Left:* Keep your eye on the ball: Pat Lindsay (on the right) and Harry Keegan (centre) mount a rearguard action in the Roscommon defence. Roscommon goalkeeper John McDermott looks on anxiously.

*Facing page:* Shut him out. Pat Lindsay (third from right) shouts advice to Dermot Earley (second from right) as Kerry's Ger Power shoots for goal in the 1978 All-Ireland semi-final. Also pictured are Roscommon's Tom Heneghan (first from right) and Tom Donnellan (fourth from right) and Kerry's Pat Spillane (second from left), John Egan (third from left) and Bomber Liston with the beard. *Photo:* Tony Conboy

early on but I feel we lost because we weren't attacking enough. We had great attacking half-backs and on the day they did a good defensive job but we didn't use them to attack Kerry. Offaly beat Kerry in 1982 by attacking them. We had the class to do the same but we didn't.

'We were gutted afterwards especially for the supporters. They gave us a massive reception when we got home. Every year Roscommon plays in the Connacht Championship there's an expectation that we can do something significant. The Roscommon supporters really rally behind the team as was shown in Ennis in 2006 when Roscommon beat Kerry in the replay of the All-Ireland minor final. The atmosphere was incredible and judging by the massive traffic jam on the way home from the game, every man, woman and child in the county was at the game. That Roscommon team played football the way I think it should be played: with great support play, no fouling and enormous commitment.'

Sligo shocked Roscommon in the first round of the Connacht Championship in 1981. 'We were complacent and I think by that stage some of the hunger had gone out of the team.'

Roscommon never matched the performances of 1980 again and Lindsay retired in 1985 after losing the Connnacht final to Mayo. A revealing insight into the man is that the biggest regret from his career is not losing the All-Ireland.

'We played Galway in the 1977 Connacht final and I was marking the great Jimmy Duggan who had won an All-Ireland medal in 1966. I played a very negative game on him. I was pulling his jersey and tripping him. I was ashamed that I had played such a negative game on such a wonderful player and such a gentleman. I got to know him afterwards and apologised for my performance that day.'

Not all his opponents were as gracious. 'I was playing a club game against Kilmore and was being my normal awkward self when I came out for the ball and accidentally knocked my opponent on to the mucky ground. He shouted up at me: "Lindsay you're a dead man!" I thought it was very funny. The guy was all talk though and didn't lay a finger on me.'

A trip to America as an All-Star replacement in 1975 gave Lindsay some of his favourite moments.

'We were managed by Seán Purcell. Seán called out the team before the first game and announced that he was playing centre-half-forward. That got a great laugh but Seán turned on us and said in all earnestness: What's so funny, lads?" Because it was Seán Purcell everybody wanted to play their best.

'Two footballers stood out for me on that trip: Frank McGuigan and Peter McGinnity. They were just incredibly talented. Frank was only the second player in history to play inter-county football at Minor, Under-21, Junior, and Senior levels in the one year. The first was Roscommon's Dermot Earley. Frank was probably the most gifted player I ever saw though he would probably be the first to admit he was never a hundred per cent fit. He loved life! I roomed with Frank for a while. It was an education! One time we stood out all night and in the morning we went to a diner for breakfast. We had a massive fry-up. A very nice waitress came over and asked if we had enjoyed our meal. Frank was a big man and he replied: "It was so good, I'll have the same again!"

When asked to select his dream team Pat prefaced his choices with the following observations:

'There have been all kinds of dream teams selected in the past but I decided to pick a team of the greatest players never to win an All-Ireland medal in my time because these great players deserve due recognition. Take Harry Keegan, for instance, who I played beside for so long. He was one of the greats. He was very fast, great to tackle, had great positional sense and could make great surging runs that would lift the crowd. I had two main selection headaches. I was really tempted to include Barnes Murphy at centre-half-back but Tommy Joe Gilmore was such a great player too. However, the one spot that really caused me to agonise was the number fifteen shirt. I was torn between Peter McGinnity and Mick Finneran. Although he played most of his football at midfield and half-forward Peter was such a good player he could have slotted in anywhere – as all the great players can.

'I picked Gay Sheeran because he was so good for so long. Mick Finneran, though, only really played for four years but I had to pick him because he had such skill. He first announced himself to us in the Connacht championship in 1977 when he came on as a sub against Mayo, having played earlier in the minor match. Just as Dermot Earley, an icon of the GAA, was placing the ball for a long distance free this young whippersnapper came running beside him and whispered to Dermot: "Give the ball to me and I will give it back to you." Dermot did as he was ordered, taking a quick free to Mick, and got the ball back much closer to the goal and slotted it over the bar.

'Although he had incredible skill and the best sidestep and dummy I ever saw Mick was not know for his work rate. In 1978 though I saw him playing against Mayo in an Under-21 match and he was turning up in midfield and the half-back line. He was playing like Pat Spillane! Another very clear memory I have of him is against Down in Newry in a challenge match. We put him as a raw eighteen-year-old in at full-forward on the Down and Ulster full-back at the time. Mick gave him the mother and father of all roastings and scored six points in the first half. All he needed was a yard and the ball was over the bar. He got RTÉ's goal of the season in 1979 in the All-Ireland semi-final against Dublin. The great pity for Roscommon football was that he gave it up so quickly because he was an outstanding talent and if you matched his flair with a fraction of Dermot Earley's dedication, you would have had one of the all time greats.'

1. Gay Sheeran
(Roscommon)

2. Harry Keegan　　　3. Seamus Quinn　　　4. Seamus McHugh
(Roscommon)　　　　　(Leitrim)　　　　　　(Galway)

5. Johnny Hughes　　　6. T. J. Gilmore　　　7. Danny Murray
(Galway)　　　　　　　(Galway)　　　　　　　(Roscommon)

8. Dermot Earley　　　　　　9. Willie Joe Padden
(Roscommon)　　　　　　　　(Mayo)

10. Mickey Martin　　　11. Jimmy Duggan　　　12. Micheál Kearins
(Leitrim)　　　　　　　(Galway)　　　　　　　(Sligo)

13. Tony McManus　　　14. Frank McGuigan　　　15. Mick Finneran
(Roscommon)　　　　　　(Tyrone)　　　　　　　(Roscommon)

# From Mayo to Galway via Sligo

## Peter Ford

Although Peter Ford is best known for his achievements in Gaelic football he first came to prominence in another sport.

'When I was sixteen and seventeen I won Irish boxing titles and was given a boxing scholarship by Cospoir, which was like today's Sports Council and I was put under the tutalage of Mick Dowling. Most weekends I would take the train to Dublin and stay with Mick, which was a great experience.

'My father, Bob won an All-Ireland junior hurling medal with Galway but when he was twenty-one or twenty-two he sustained a bad eye injury and was sent to hospital in the city and told him he needed to have his eye taken out the next day. A nurse, though, told him not to let them take out the eye so my father sneaked out of the hospital in the middle of the night. The nurse looked after him outside the hospital and six months later his eyesight returned. Then he went to South Africa for five years and when he returned his hurling career was over.

'My father died when I was eighteen, my mother having died seven years earlier. I think I had been boxing just to make him proud. At the time I was training ten or twelve times a week whereas the footballers were only training three times a week and they seemed to be having great craic so I decided to give up the boxing and concentrate on the football.'

In 1983 Ford won an All-Ireland on the pitch when he starred in Mayo's Under-21 triumph. Five years earlier he had won his first All-Ireland medal.

'I was a sub on the Mayo team that won the All-Ireland minor title. It's not the same when you are not on the team but it was nice to happen when you are just sixteen. I had two more years as a minor. In '79 I marked Barney Rock when we lost to Dublin in the All-Ireland semi-final and we lost to Derry the following year at the same stage.

'At the start of '83 I was captain and full-back of the Under-21s but I went to America for the summer and lost both my place and the captaincy.

I was back for the semi-final and played at corner-back. Our captain was Eddie Gibbons who was sent off in the final and as a result could not be presented with the cup.'

The team was managed by John O'Mahony but it was not Ford's first encounter with his future boss on the senior team.

'I had marked John a few times in club games. He was playing full-forward at that stage and was a good player and free-taker. He was coming to the end of his career and I was a little faster than him then! As a manager, John had a very strong presence and was very organised. Although we trained well he made the whole thing a very enjoyable experience.'

Having made the senior panel that year in 1984 Ford became a regular in the Mayo defence.

'Liam O'Neill was manager then and he brought a lot of professionalism to the set-up. Before that things had been more laissez-faire. In 1985 we beat Roscommon in the Connacht final. Roscommon had given us a few bad beatings down the years so we were really determined to see them off. I had no fears about playing Dublin in the All-Ireland semi-final because we had played them as minors and when you are young you don't think you will be beaten. We gave away two bad goals in the replay and that finished us despite Padraig Brogan scoring the famous "wonder goal".'

For many people the abiding memory from the first game was the infamous 'John Finn incident' in which the Mayo half-back sustained a broken jaw in an off-the-field challenge.

'When you think back it says a lot about John that he continued to play on even though his jaw was broken. He was on the other side of the field from the ball when he was attacked. To be honest it didn't affect us at all because we were not thinking about him but focusing on winning the game. John never spoke about it at all so it didn't hype us up for the replay. It was much later before it became common knowledge who the "culprit" was but typical of the time no action was ever taken by the GAA against the offending player.

'In both '87 and '88 I had a back injury and was unable to play. John O'Mahony had taken over for the '88 Championship and had pressed me to get involved but I couldn't. In '89 I was boxing again and was beaten in the Irish senior final.

'That year we beat Roscommon in the Connacht final replay after extra-time. Tony McManus was on fire that day and scored 2-5 for Roscommon. That morning I had a bad quad muscle injury and told the boys that I wasn't playing but John O'Mahony insisted I did. I got a pain-killing injection and couldn't feel anything. I was petrified at the start of the

match that the leg wouldn't last but it did and I woke up the next morning and my leg was fine.

'Johnno always told us not to read the papers before big games but I did the morning of the All-Ireland semi-final and the headline in one was "McKenna holds the key". I decided that there was no way my opponent Eugene McKenna was going to be the key. That was the lift I needed to fire me up to make sure he did not pose a threat. In fact T. J. Kilgallon was playing at centre-half-back that day which was very unusual for him and when Eugene switched to centre-half-forward and Damien O'Hagan went full-forward, T. J. asked to go in full-back because he was holding Damien so well, even though it's a very different position and one he never played in before. I enjoyed the opportunity to go on the attack at centre-back.'

Ford's enduring memory of the All-Ireland final is not the most obvious one.

'There was a picture of me in the paper next day with tears in my eyes but my abiding memory will always be the Cork captain Dinny Allen's speech when he was presented with the Cup. He came out with a load of bollocks. He spent nearly all his speech lacerating the media. I couldn't believe that after winning the All-Ireland that was all that was on his mind. If we had won it would have been a very different story.'

Mayo had great expectations the following year. Not for the first time their hopes were dashed.

'In 1990 we played sh*t and were arrogant. We had a trial game before we played Galway in the Connacht Championship and the B team beat us badly. Galway too hammered the daylights out of us and I marked a guy I didn't rate which was part of the malaise and he gave me a hard time. With that level of complacency our chance of progressing from '89 was gone.'

Significantly, the narrow loss in the All-Ireland semi-final to Donegal in 1992 is not one of the big regrets of his career. The immediate aftermath weighs more heavily on his mind.

'A lot of controversy was generated by the stories that surfaced about the training methods of our manager Brian McDonald. Brian's family got a lot of abuse afterwards. That should not have happened. I was captain that year and whatever grievances we might have had with Brian's training methods, there's no way they should all have got into the media in that

*Left:* Pensive Peter: Peter Ford looks on as Galway take on Mayo in the 2007 Connacht Championship. *Photo:* Connacht Tribune.

fashion nor should Brian have got such a pilloring. I didn't realise 'til later how much Brian's family had suffered, through abusive phone-calls because of the controversy and I still feel terrible that they had to go through it. It is one of the big regrets of my career.'

He also has a couple of regrets about the semi-final itself.

'I had a shoulder injury before the game and had to take a pain-killing injection. I was marking Tony Boyle and he did terrible damage that day. As captain, the management had promised me that no matter what happened Padraig Brogan would not be brought on as a sub even if the game was in balance because he had played for Donegal the year before and the sight of him would gee on the Donegal side. However, he was brought on with exactly the result that I had anticipated.'

Mayo fans thought that they had unearthed football's answer to Merlin the magician when Jack O'Shea took over as county manager that year.

'I was a sub in '93 and didn't really play. Jacko was very enthusiastic but people were expecting miracles and thought he had some kind of a secret ingredient from playing under Mick O'Dwyer but there is no magic formula in Kerry or in anywhere else. We were butchered in the All-Ireland semi-final and I retired.'

Ford soon found himself back in Mayo football when John Maughan made him one of his selectors. The big chance of glory came in the 1996 All-Ireland final.

'With fifteen minutes to go I could only see one result. Mayo had a comfortable lead but we tried to defend it and pushed back too far and allowed Meath to pick off their points.'

It is very evident that Ford feels a strong grievance about the replay. 'The sending offs were a complete mismatch. Liam McHale was our best player and while Colm Coyle was a fine player his loss to Meath in no way compared with the loss of Liam to us. I've heard it back since from informed sources, shall we say, that the referee had intended to send of one of the Meath midfielders but the umpire intervened and told him he had to send Coyle off because of his role in the mêlée. When we played against the breeze Liam would have been ideal for that. Nonetheless we struggled on and only lost by a point.'

The following year the Mayo management was criticised for the decision-making in the All-Ireland final defeat to Kerry.

'I stand over what we did. We played an army team about ten days before the game and Dermot Flanagan got injured. Looking back we shouldn't have played that game. Dermot was the sort of player who liked to keep fresh so we didn't push him into lots of fitness tests. We had a plan if he didn't work out and had prepared for that eventuality and had decided on the switches we would make. If we had someone on the subs of the same quality we would have brought him on straight away but we hadn't so it ended up as multiple switches rather than one.

'Maurice Fitzgerald scored three points from play that day. Pat Holmes did what any good defender is told to do in these situations. He forced him out to the sideline and normally there would be no danger but Maurice could kick points from there. It's very hard to find anybody to mark any player that good in that sort of form. It's almost freakish.'

In 2001, after spending several years teaching in Sligo and gaining a reputation as a coach in Summerhill at schools level as well as earning success in Mayo at club level, Ford found himself managing Sligo.

'I was half-hoping that I might get the Mayo job but I had three brilliant years with Sligo. We lost by a point to Mayo in the Connacht Championship, having missed a penalty in Castlebar in 2001 but I suppose the first highlight came some weeks later against Kildare. They had been in an All-Ireland final three years before and had won another Leinster title after that and, under Mick O'Dwyer, were one of the glamour teams. On the seventh of July we were the first Sligo team to win in Croke Park. Even though we lost, playing Dublin then in Croke Park was a wonderful occasion. I suppose one of the real high points came when we beat Tyrone the following year as they were the team of stars and had so many household names. We then went on to draw with Armagh and were unlucky to lose the replay. We could have got a penalty in the last minute.

'We were punching above our weight. We are performing well, getting great support and there was great goodwill to us in the county. We also had great players. Everyone knows about Eamonn O'Hara but Dessie Sloyan was a really great forward who would consistently score for you and we had other great fellas like Kieran Quinn and John McPartland. The team brought a lot of enjoyment and it was a happy county in 2002 and there was no bitterness when we lost.

'In 2003 things started to go wrong and within the local media in Sligo there was a section that turned on us. That didn't help and does affect the players. We had three or four injuries to key players and, as Tyrone have shown in recent years, no matter how much talent you have you can't win without your big players. The desire wasn't as strong and we had become complacent.'

Having raised Sligo up to new heights Ford found himself filling the large shoes of John O'Mahony as Galway manager.

'My father was from Galway and I had gone to college there but I also took the job because I thought I had the chance to win an All-Ireland. We won a Connacht title and an Under-21 All-Ireland in 2005. We lost the first three League matches in 2006 and that put a strain on us and an element within the local media turned on us. Players started to have doubts. Although we qualified for the League final, things did not go to plan in the Championship. The nadir was losing to Westmeath in the qualifiers. I was absolutely disgusted. A part of me wanted to walk away after that but I felt that would be the cowardly thing to do. I wanted to try and put things right. In 2007 we were really right for the match against Mayo. The older lads were really psyched to put one over on John O'Mahony. We were never able to get up for it again that summer in the same way and losing to Sligo in the Connacht final is not acceptable in Galway. Losing to Meath in the Qualifiers was a real downer. I accepted the blame for the defeats but my three years were up and it was time to move on.'

Having served under both John O'Mahony and John Maughan, Ford is ideally equipped to assess the respective merits of each manager.

'They are similar in the sense that they are both strong characters who bring a big work ethic, great self-belief and very good organisation to the job. They are very dissimilar, though, in the way they operate. John Maughan is more in people's faces, John O'Mahony less so. Both styles will suit some players better than others. Maughan is an extrovert, who enjoys the hype and likes to blow things up. O'Mahony likes to keep a low profile and stay out of the limelight. O'Mahony is more into psychology, Maughan is more into tactics.'

Ford's reply is immediate when asked about the frustrations of being a manager.

'When you are building up to a big game and have your plans based around a player or players it is incredibly frustrating when they get injured. It's a killer on morale. Another problem is that some players play the way the want to anyway, no matter what you say, often to the detriment of the team. The dilemma is whether you are better off without them.'

A subtext in Ford's review of his career is the role of the media. 'If a main GAA figure in the local media is constantly critical of the team or individual players it has a very negative effect. Players have wives, girlfriends, fathers and mothers. They find constant negative articles upsetting which in turn affects the players in question. These are guys who make huge sacrifices to train and they find it frustrating to read a constant level of abuse.'

Is Ford himself badly affected by media criticism?

'What kills me is losing. After losing some of the big games in

Galway I wouldn't want to show my face in the county for days, sometimes weeks. I put on a brave face in interviews after the games but I took the defeats very badly. I was very depressed for weeks after some of our bad losses.'

Ford selected a dream team of Connacht players from 1980 onwards. Given that the ties of friendship with many of them is so strong he omitted Mayo players from consideration. Although he is out of position he was particularly anxious to include Paul Clancy as he considers him a 'most underrated player'.

1. Martin McNamara
(Galway)

2. Harry Keegan
(Roscommon)

3. Gary Fahy
(Galway)

4. Seamus McHugh
(Galway)

5. Declan Meehan
(Galway)

6. Tomás Mannion
( Galway)

7. Seán Óg de Paor
(Galway)

8. Dermot Earley
(Roscommon)

9. Kevin Walsh
(Galway)

10. Eamonn O'Hara
(Sligo)

11. Ja Fallon
(Galway)

12. Michael Donnellan
(Galway)

13. Paul Clancy
(Galway)

14. Padraig Joyce
(Galway)

15. Tony McManus
(Roscommon)

Midfield Maestros

# Earley to Rise

## Dermot Earley

Motto of a Young Footballer:
*To play the game with skill and flair*
*But most of all to play it fairly*
*To learn to win and lose with grace*
*To play the game like Dermot Earley.*

For Dermot Earley, there were advantages and disadvantages in having his father as a teacher. The advantages were that he could call his father whenever he needed assistance with homework or required points of clarification. The disadvantages were that he could never skip on homework or use the classic excuse: 'Please Sir, I forgot my copy.' There was one time that Dermot Earley realised that his father often saw more than he let on at home.

'We were given particularly difficult sums involving addition, subtraction, multiplication and division. If you made a mistake in the beginning you got the whole thing wrong. My father was watching me that night but did not make any comment. The next day he was correcting the sums when he asked all those who got them right to put up their hands. I put up my hand. He walked down and asked, "Is that the answer on the board?" I said no. He said nothing more until later that evening. All the lads were gathering outside to play football. I was all set to go out to play with them but my father said: "Come here you. Where are you going?"

"Out to play football."

"No you are not. You told me a lie today. You are staying in all evening."

'He never said anything else. I stood at the window watching the lads going to the match. It was the longest two hours that I ever spent. I will never forget it. It taught me a lesson. Never tell a lie. We often talked

*Preceding page:* One that got away: Willie Joe Padden (first on left) looks on helplessly as Roscommon's Paul Earley leaps like a lord against Mayo in the 1991 Connacht final. *Photo:* Roscommon Champion/*Gerard O'Loughlin*

about it afterwards. When I had kids of my own and was chastising them for telling lies he would say: "Your daddy will tell you all about telling lies." It was the right way to do it. It extracted the maximum punishment and he never laid a finger on me.'

Having made his debut for Roscommon in 1965 as a seventeen-year-old Earley learned a lot when he won his first Railway Cup medal for Connacht in 1967.

'I later asked Johnny Geraghty, the Galway goalie of the three-in-a-row team, how he knew that side was crumbling. He replied: "I remember coming into training one day and one player did not have his boots polished. I put that down as the beginning of the end." I learned that the preparation that was required was total. When that did not happen the team went downhill.'

Earley won All-Stars in 1974 and 1979 and a National League medal in 1979 but, unusually, found himself embroiled in controversy in 1977 in the All-Ireland semi-final against Armagh. With the score tied at Armagh 3-9 Roscommon 2-12, Earley faced up to a long-distance free, the last kick

*Below (left):* Back off. Dermot Earley backs into Galway's T.J. Gilmore in the 1974 Connacht final. *(right):* Earley defeat. Dermot Earley (left of pic) loses out to the Cork defence in a League clash. *Photos:* Tony Conboy.

of the game. Gerry O'Neill (brother of former Celtic manager, Martin), the Armagh trainer, ran across the field in front of him and shouted something at him. The kick sailed high and wide. There was much press comment on the 'O'Neill-Earley' incident in the following days. In his column in the Evening Press Con Houlihan offered two All-Ireland tickets to the person who could tell him what O'Neill said to Earley. The Roscommon star was not unduly distracted: 'I had no idea what he said to me that time. I wasn't even aware that he was talking to me. All I wanted to do was drill the ball over the bar.'

In June 2007, Earley became Chief of the Staff of the Irish defence forces. His sporting interest was to help him professionally. 'During my playing days I was part of a peacekeeping mission with the UN on the Golan Heights. Some of my colleagues and I went on an inspection on the Syrian side of the Golan Heights and we went to a particular camp where the commander would not allow us to inspect. There was consternation when we were discovered and we were marched to the commander's tent.

'There he had pictures of many beautiful girls on the wall and he also had pictures of great soccer players, particularly goalkeepers, from England and Europe. Immediately the conversation turned to football. The next thing, a football was produced from behind a desk. The commander explained that he was a goalkeeper himself and he invited us outside to show off his skills. Goals were set up and a penalty competition was introduced. As the commander stood tall and erect in the goal, his "goalposts" were two stones, just like we used in the west of Ireland years ago.

'The event had caught the imagination of the camp and everybody was crowding around the "pitch". There was a great carnival atmosphere. An Irish officer was designated as the penalty taker. One of the other observers whispered into his ear saying, "Perhaps this an occasion you should miss." The penalty taker faced a tricky situation. If he scored the commander would be embarrassed. He did not look very agile. His ability might not match his interest. The easiest kick for a goalie to save is a shot

*Right:* Commander-in-chief: Head of the Defence Forces Dermot Earley greets Taoiseach Bertie Ahern at Defence Forces Headquarters in 2007.

that is waist high and is right in the centre of the goal. The ball can be hit very hard but all the keeper has to do is to stand up straight and put up his hands. With this in mind the Irish officer blasted the ball straight at the commander. It looked like a great save and he was delighted. All the Syrian soldiers were ecstatic; it was like winning the World Cup itself.

'That penalty save completely diffused a potentially difficult decision. The commander was higher in the estimation of his troops than ever before and savoured his moment of glory. The UN officers left, confident in the knowledge that relations would be smoother with that particular camp in the foreseeable future.'

After he retired from football, Earley managed the Roscommon team for two years. During the winter he trained the Dublin-based players in the Phoenix Park. They trained there a few days after Earley substituted a player in a game. The player in question was unhappy with his substitution. After training the squad normally went to the Aisling Hotel for a meal. However, before joining the others Earley and the player were sitting outside the hotel in the car having a very serious discussion about the player and his future with the team. There was a loud rap on the window. They turned around to see a lady of the night asking them, 'Would you like a good time?'

After his stint in charge of Roscommon, Earley took over as manager of the Kildare team from Mick O'Dwyer. Kildare's problem has always been the lack of scoring forwards. Shortly after his appointment Earley was up on the roof of his two-storey house in Newbridge painting his chimney when a Kildare fan passed by on his bicycle and shouted up at him, 'Are you looking for forwards?'

Earley's dream team from his playing days, excluding Roscommon players, is:

1. Billy Morgan
(Cork)

| 2. Enda Colleran | 3. Jack Quinn | 4. Tom O'Hare |
| (Galway) | (Meath) | (Down) |

| 5. Páidí Ó Sé | 6. Nicholas Clavin | 7. Martin Newell |
| (Kerry) | ( Offaly) | (Galway) |

| 8. Jimmy Duggan | 9. Jack O'Shea |
| (Galway) | (Kerry) |

| 10. Matt Connor | 11. Denis 'Ogie' Moran | 12. Pat Spillane |
| (Offaly) | (Kerry) | (Kerry) |

| 13. Mike Sheehy | 14. Seán O'Neill | 15. John Egan |
| (Kerry) | (Down) | (Kerry) |

# Tunnel Vision

## Brian Talty

B rian Talty has already chosen his epitaph. It is an apt one, given that he experienced the fate so many times as a player, as a coach and selector: 'We were beaten by a point.'

Football almost caused a major split in his family in his childhood. 'Growing up in Tuam I wanted to go to secondary school in Tuam CBS like the rest of my friends but my father wanted me to go to St Jarlath's College. In the end he promised me a tracksuit if I went to Jarlath's and a tracksuit was a huge thing back in the late sixties so that's what persuaded me to go. Mind you, I never got the tracksuit! Football was like a religion in Jarlath's and it really helped me develop as a footballer.

'My dad was heavily involved in the club in Tuam and because of that I got the chance to watch the Galway three-in-a-row team train. I got to know them and became close to Johnny Geraghty. For that reason, I initially started as a goalkeeper in Jarlath's.'

Talty did not come close to Johnny Geraghty's standards as a goalkeeper and found his home in midfield as he won the ultimate prize in college football – the Hogan Cup – with Jarlath's. Another All-Ireland medal, this time at club level, quickly followed when he moved to Thomond College to train as a PE teacher. His teammates included such luminaries as Pat Spillane and the player whose name was destined to become inextricably linked to his own, Brian Mullins.

'It was great to play on a team of stars and win an All-Ireland but, long-term, one of the biggest influences on me there, in terms of my own coaching style to this day, was our coach Dave Weldrick who some people will remember as a panelist on The Sunday Game in the late '70s.'

In 1976 Talty won his first senior Connacht medal when Galway beat Roscommon in a replay.

'Dermot Earley was away on peacekeeping duty that year and missed the Championship. I was always hoping after that he would be in the Lebanon or somewhere whenever we played Roscommon in the Championship!'

The following year, though, Earley was back in the fold and Roscommon beat Galway by a point in the Connacht final.

'My father was in the stand that day. A Galway fan near him was shouting: "Take him off" about me. When I got a goal he quietened down a bit. When I got a second goal and a point Dad turned around and said to him: "Do you still want to take him off?"'

The disappointments in the Connacht Championship in those years were offset by victories in the Gael Linn competition.

'The prize for winning it was a trip to New York so that's why we put more into winning it than the Connacht Championship! We had some great times on those trips. My abiding memory is of rooming once with Billy Joyce. We were staying in the Taft Hotel. It should've been called the Daft Hotel! One day, Billy was lying on the bed when of our teammates came rushing into the room in a state of high excitement shouting: 'I've just got the news that I've won an All-Star."

Billy coolly looked up him and said: "Didn't I tell you that you'd get one?" Our colleague beamed and said: "You did." Then modesty took over and he added: "I didn't deserve one." Billy's response was immediate: "Correct."'

1977 was the beginning of a four-in-a-row of Connacht titles for Roscommon, so it was 1981 before Galway claimed another major title when they comprehensively beat Roscommon to win the National League title. Talty sees the win as a mixed blessing.

'We got great plaudits for winning by playing a traditional catch-and-kick style of game. The problem was that for the next two years we stuck rigidly to that approach and in the All-Ireland final in 1983 when a variation in our tactics was called for we didn't have a plan B and we paid a big price for that failure in that game.'

Although Mayo ambushed them in 1981 Galway crushed their old rivals in the Connacht final in '82. Not for the last time, Talty and his colleagues found themselves dragged into controversy.

'There was a by-election on at the time in one of the Galway constituencies and we got into hot water with the GAA authorities for shaking hands with the Fianna Fáil candidate Noel Tracey. What else were we to do when he came into the dressing room and held out his hand to us? To guys like me from Tuam, our real rivalry is with Mayo because we border them whereas the guys close to the Roscommon border think our real rivalry is with them. So beating Mayo was a sweet feeling.'

Galway had the winning of the All-Ireland semi-final against Offaly but missed chance after chance, especially very kickable frees. 'If we had a free-taker of the calibre of Matt Connor we would have won at least one All-Ireland. Guys like Stephen Joyce and Gay McManus worked so hard in training on their frees but you can't replicate the pressure of an All-Ireland semi-final in Croke Park in training. Had we beat Offaly that year we mightn't have beaten Kerry in the final but it would have been a great preparation for playing the Dubs in the All-Ireland the following year.'

In 1983, Galway showed all the signs of a good team when qualifying for the All-Ireland final – they won without playing well.

'Living and working in Dublin I was trying to keep away from the hype as much as possible which wasn't easy. I was having a tough year. I had a stomach injury for most of the season and was spending a lot of time on the physio's table. Nowadays there would probably be a name for the condition like "Gilmore's groin" but back then there wasn't much understanding. My mother said: "It's all in your head."

'Billy Joyce never believed in injuries and met me one day when I was going to see someone who had a good reputation for dealing with my condition. When I told him where I was going he said: "For Jaysus' sake, if I told you there was an auld wan with a magic cure you'd go to her." Years later I met him in Tuam on crutches and asked him what had happened. He told me that he was getting out of his car and he tore his Achilles tendon. I told him it was all in his head!'

On the day of the final, it was a different kind of injury to Talty that would be forever imprinted on the public consciousness.

'I remember waking up on the morning and being very disappointed that it was such a wet and windy day because I knew it was going to spoil the match a bit. The game ended with us having fourteen players and Dublin only twelve but it could have been six versus six because there were so many belts flying in. Despite the extra men, we still lost because we missed so many easy chances. The Dubs manager Kevin Heffernan got his tactics right. He withdrew everyone else from the full-forward line and left Joe McNally up on his own. With the wet and windy conditions it was the sort of day you could crowd your opponents. We didn't have the tactical variation to respond to the circumstances or even the conditions.'

The boil must be lanced. It is time to hear what really happened with Brian Mullins.

'From a personal point of view it was a massive disappointment to become embroiled in the worst controversy of my career. That was the hardest part for me, not that Brian nearly took the top of my head off! If you look back on it on TV you will see he really made contact with me! Brian was one of my heroes when I went to Thomond College and played with him. When I got married in 1980 Brian was at our wedding. I was on my honeymoon when he had that terrible car accident. As he started to rehab I played soccer with him so I knew at first hand how far he had to travel to get back to the level he did. Nobody else would put themselves through what he did to get back to the very top. I'm sorry that his achievement in getting back was tainted a bit by him being sent off in an All-Ireland final and especially because it was for striking me. I think what Dublin did that day was incredible but it is such a pity for their own sake that the controversy took away from what they did. It was heroic stuff.'

Twenty-five years on, the story of what happened in the tunnel continues to be shrouded in mystery. Talty will take the full truth to his grave.

'There was a bit of pushing and shoving and I was struck. The real damage to me was not that one nor Brian's one but after the sending off I was charging through to the Dublin goal when P. J. Buckley caught me on the head. Having said that, after Brian and P. J., I could have done without the one in the tunnel! In the dressing room Billy Joyce asked me if I was OK to continue and while I said I was the selectors saw it differently.'

There was unfinished business to be resolved afterwards.

'There was a lot of tension the next day when the two teams met up for the meal which was the tradition at the time. A few words were exchanged! Joe McNally got up to sing "The Fields of Athenry". I remember thinking: "Jesus Christ, wouldn't I love to kill you!"

'Brian and I went outside in the car park to have a conversation. What sticks in my memory is what when Brian was coming towards to me I was thinking: "I hope he's not going to strike me again!" He told me and he was probably right that I was pulling and dragging out of him and that is why he reacted. To be honest, I'm not sure if the talk accomplished anything. My other vivid memory is seeing the way Galway's Stephen Kineavy and Dublin's Mick Holden, Lord have mercy on him, blocked off the car park and nobody was going to disturb us.'

Talty is thankful for small mercies.

'Brian was teaching in Kilbarrack at the time. Before I got my teaching job in St David's Artane I had done an interview in Brian's school but didn't get it. Imagine if I had to work with him as well while the controversy was raging!'

A complication for Talty was that he was playing his club football in Dublin.

'The Parnells fellas thought I was there just to take the clatters! A lot of club players decided to take out their frustration on me after that All-Ireland. As long as we won championships I didn't care. It was my first year with Parnells. At the end of the year the club gives an award to anyone who has played in the All-Ireland during the year. There was no one from Dublin that year so I was the only one to receive one. I think I pulled a hood over my head to collect mine!'

Talty is philosophical as he looks back at the controversy a quarter of a century on.

'Since I first played for Jarlath's and had setbacks my attitude has always been that once the Tuam Herald is out on the Thursday and reports on the event it's over and it's time to move on. '83 was a bit different because it took three weeks of Tuam Heralds before I was over it! Thanks be to God twenty-five years have passed and there have been a lot of Tuam Heralds and I am friends with Brian again. Kieran Duff, who was also sent off that day, and I work with each other in the Dublin set-up. I would have never thought then that twenty-five years on I would be going to Newcastle to see a soccer match with Kieran!'

Talty's trips to America with the All-Stars did create some lasting friendships.

'Frank McGuigan was a great tourist. He'd play games after having had a few pints and still go out and grab great balls out of the air. I always wondered what he'd be like if he had no pints!

'At the time instead of us staying in hotels we often stayed with host families. On one of those trips Tom Prendergast from Laois went to stay in an apartment owned by a Laois man. There was a foreign man staying there and Tom decided to stay with some friends. The next day when we went to play our match there was police everywhere. The guy staying in Tom's apartment had been shot dead there the night before and Tom was a suspect. We often wondered what would have happened if Tom had stayed there that night.

'One of my clearest memories is of playing at centre-field in Gaelic Park against Kerry. They had come up with this revolutionary move at the time, everybody does it now, which involves the midfielders switching sides. Tom Spillane had just come on the scene and I remember looking at my midfield partner Moses Coffey and saying: "What the f**k is happening?" The second match was in San Francisco and before it Moses came to me and said: "Don't worry. I will sort things out today." The first ball that came our way I heard a screech of pain and saw Tom Spillane sprawled out on the ground. There was no more crossing over that day!'

Even before his playing career had finished Talty had made his mark as a coach. In 1986 he coached Saint David's to an All-Ireland A Colleges final.

'We were beaten in the final by Colman's of Newry. James McCartan was the man who beat us. He had a massive game.'

In 1988 Talty captained and coached Parnells to a Dublin and Leinster title only to lose to Nemo Rangers in the All-Ireland semi-final . . . by a point. He also coached Sylvesters to a Dublin title. In addition he coached the Dublin-based Roscommon players when they won a Connacht title in 2001. His coaching career has not been without controversy and another tunnel incident haunts him.

'I was coaching St Jude's and after a game in Parnell Park there was a row in the tunnel and the officials decided that the best way to deal with it was to turn off the light. At that stage I felt a punch being thrown over my head. When the lights were turned on I was standing behind the referee and had a big smile on my face but the ref had been punched. The referee reported me for striking and I was suspended for three months. I know who threw the punch and he got away scot free. I'm not sure was he trying to punch me or the ref. I'm still protesting my innocence to the County Board.'

Nonetheless, his club career in Dublin also brought plaudits from the corridors of power, especially after steering Parnells to victory.

Pillar Caffrey brought Talty into the Dublin set-up as one of his selectors. One of the criticisms of the Dublin team is that they have been involved with 'sledging' or verbal attacks on their opponents. To many it is a blot on the game.

'The criticism of the Dublin lads is absolutely unfair. When fellas are hit off the ball would people prefer if they responded by giving their opponent a clatter? In the heat of the moment Mark Vaughan, Alan Brogan

*Below: (left)* A telegram from An Taoiseach; *(right)* The Life of Brian: Brian Talty shares a greeting with Charlie Haughey after they were introduced by Br Tommy McDonnell (second from left) in St David's Artane in 1991.

Dear Brian,

Please accept my sincere congratulations on your great win on Saturday last.

I would like you to pass on my good wishes to each member of the team on their superb performance and look forward to another good year in 1989.

With best wishes and kindest regards,

Yours sincerely,

Taoiseach.

Oifig an Taoisigh, Tithe an Rialtais Baile Átha Cliath 2.
Office of the Taoiseach, Government Buildings, Dublin 2.

and Kevin Bonner reacted to being provoked over long periods.'

Laughter regularly punctuates Talty's .conversation. Perhaps that explains why he looks as if he set to become the Peter Pan of Gaelic football. The laughter is accentuated whenever Billy Joyce is brought into the conversation.

'Once, before we played a big match in Croke Park, Billy took us by surprise by asking: "Did ye ring the airport?" I didn't know what he was talking about and asked him why would we ring the airport. He replied: "To tell them not to have airplanes flying over Croke Park. I'm going to be jumping so high I don't want to be in collision with them."

'When we were getting beaten in midfield by a particular player, Billy would turn to me and say: "Time to take the chopper out." The next ball that came our way you would hear a thud and a sigh of pain. We were playing Roscommon in Pearse Stadium and it was an atrocious wet day. Before the throw-in one of their midfielders said to Billy: "'Tis an awful day for football." Billy looked at him and said: "You don't have to worry about it. You won't be out in it very long." He was right!'

Talty's dream team from his own era is:

1. Martin Furlong
(Offaly)

2. Robbie O'Malley    3. John O'Keeffe    4. Mick Lyons
(Meath)          (Kerry)          (Meath)

5. Páidí Ó Sé    6. T. J. Gilmore    7. Johnny Hughes
(Kerry)          (Galway)          (Galway)

8. Jack O'Shea          9. Brian Mullins
(Kerry)                (Dublin)

10. Pat Spillane    11. Dermot Earley    12. Peter McGinnity
(Kerry)          (Roscommon)          (Fermanagh)

13. Mike Sheehy    14. Frank McGuigan    15. Tony McManus
(Kerry)          (Tyrone)          (Roscommon)

# Blood and Bandages

## Willie Joe Padden

*'Will Galway bate Mayo?*
*Not if they have Willie Joe'*
(from 'Hay Wrap' by The Saw Doctors)

Like the great John Joe O'Reilly, Willie Joe Padden is one of the elite group of footballers who have been immortalised in a song. The Mayo midfielder takes it all in his stride.

'I know some of the lads in the band and, sadly, I think they chose me just because my name ryhmed with Mayo not because of my brilliance on the pitch! There have been a few strange moments. Five or six years ago this American came over to visit Ireland just because he was a massive fan of The Saw Doctors and as soon as he came in the door of the bar I had in Castlebar at the time he asked me: "Hey man, are you the guy in the song?"

Having made his debut with Mayo in 1977 while still in his teens, Padden found himself playing in the National League final against All-Ireland champions in Dublin in 1978.

'I was nineteen and started at full-forward marking Seán Doherty and then was switched to midfield on Brian Mullins. It was a bit intimidating but I had to get on with it. It was a very good game. I think it ended up 2-18 to 2-13 but we lost. That was a major step up for the county as we hadn't been in a senior final for years, despite Under-21 All-Irelands in '74 and a minor All-Ireland in 1978.

'At the time Mayo football was on a downer. People outside the county don't always realise just how football mad Mayo is. I was always very aware of the tradition especially the '50 and '51 All-Ireland winning teams. Names like Seán Flanagan, Tom Langan and Padraic Carney are legends around here because of what they did for the county.

'We didn't win the Connacht Championship in the 1970s but we were affected by what was going on all round us. Kerry and Dublin had raised the bar. If you were really serious about playing football and if you

*Above:* Out of my way: Willie Joe Padden (centre) brushes aside Cork's Conor Counihan (far right) in the 1989 All-Ireland final.

wanted to be in the All-Ireland series, you went from basically two nights' training a week to four nights a week. We hadn't been doing the training that was required to make a breakthrough at national level.'

The joy of a Connacht title in 1981 quickly turned into bitter disappointment when Mayo faced Kerry in the All-Ireland semi-final.

'They were at their pinnacle. We were probably well in the game around half-time but in the second half it was a no-show as far as we were concerned. We got beaten by sixteen points in the end. Although it was very disappointing to lose it might have been a blessing in disguise because it really showed us that we had an awful lot to do to be able to compete with the Kerrys and Dublins of the time.'

Mayo's philosophy of the game is a source of pride for Padden.

'Down through the years we have provided some very good entertainment. Unfortunately that's no good to you when you want results. But there would be a great flair in Mayo football. I sometimes think you might be able to compare us to the French rugby team. When we play football to our maximum we are very attractive. We've always had very talented footballers.'

Some players have their careers defined in moments. Willie Joe Padden is such a player. In the All-Ireland semi-final in 1989 against Tyrone he was forced to the sideline with a dangerous cut to his head. In one of the most iconic images in the history of the GAA he later returned to the fray, covered in blood, his head wrapped in a bandage, his shirt splattered in blood.

'Everybody had written us of before the match. I got an injury. I'm not too sure which Tyrone player it was. He was going for a ball and he hit his knee off my head and I got a few stitches in it. You don't mind getting a few things like that as long as you win the game. It was our first experience of getting to a final after all our endeavours from the previous years. From our point of view and from the spectators' point of view, it was a great period because we were basking in the build-up to the final, especially being in our first All-Ireland for so long.

'It was one of the more open All-Irelands. Unfortunately, Jimmy Burke, our full-forward, got injured and he had to go off. That really took the wind out of our sails a bit because he was in there as a target-man and did that job very well. We were forced to re-jig the team. Having said that when we took the lead in the second half we looked as if we were in the driving seat but we got another injury and had to re-jig the team again. I think it was that cost us the game rather than a lack of concentration. We were just as well prepared as Cork so it certainly wasn't a lack of fitness. We didn't press home our initiative. We didn't get the extra couple of points up to have the cushion there for the end of the game. Cork rallied and pipped us in the end.'

The disappointment for Padden was heightened because he knew there were not many chances left for him to win a coveted All-Ireland medal.

'It's all right playing in an All-Ireland final but if you don't win no one is going to say who the runners-up were in ten years' time, if they're asked the question. I remember thinking at the time: "Am I going to get the

*Above:* Knocking on Heaven's Door: Willie Joe Padden soars to win the ball in the All-Ireland semi-final against Dublin in 1985. *Photo:* Western People/*Henry Wills*

chance to stand in Croke Park again and have another go at winning an All-Ireland?" Sadly it was not to be.'

There is an undercurrent of sadness in Padden's voice as he recalls the way his Mayo career ended in 1992.

'Jack O'Shea had taken over as manager and I suppose his reading of it was that some of the older lads had enough mileage on the clock. He decided to bring in some new blood. I felt that I still had a contribution to make to the team for another year or two, maybe as a fringe player.

When the panel was picked I wasn't included. Maybe it did hurt me a bit. I certainly found it a shock to the system, having been involved with the county for so long, because your life is built around training and playing. You do miss it. But the time comes for everyone to move on.'

In recent years, Padden has had the privilege of seeing his son, Billy Joe, line out for Mayo.

'It is nice, first of all, to see young lads interested in football and to see him playing for Mayo is something I'm proud of. The great thing is that they are still, in the main, a young team and the experience of having played in two All-Irelands will stand to them, if they ever get back to another final.'

With five Connacht medals and two All-Star awards to his name, Padden can look back at the disappointments of the past with a wry smile. 'When we played Kerry in the All-Ireland semi-final in 1981 we did well in the first half but they gave us such a hammering in the second half that our goalkeeper, Michael Webb, said to me: "Everytime I kicked out the ball I wondered would I have time to get back into the goal before the ball landed back in!"'

Padden's sharp wit was shown when he was approached by a stranger in an airport who said: 'You're a dead ringer for Ian Botham.' Quick as a flash, Willie Joe replied: 'Funny, I never get any of his cheques.' Willie Joe excluded Mayo players from his dream team but claims he could easily pick fifteen Mayo fellas who would beat any dream team! His team is:

1. John O'Leary
(Dublin)

2. Páidí Ó Sé       3. Darren Fay       4. Martin O'Connell
(Kerry)              (Meath)              (Meath)

5. Seamus Moynihan   6. Kieran McGeeney   7. Seán Óg de Paor
(Kerry)              (Armagh)             (Galway)

8. Jack O'Shea              9. Darragh Ó Sé
(Kerry)                     (Dublin)

10. Maurice Fitzgerald   11. Larry Tompkins   12. Pat Spillane
(Kerry)                   (Cork)               (Kerry)

13. Mickey Linden   14. Peter Canavan   15. Colm 'Gooch' Cooper
(Down)               (Tyrone)            (Kerry)

# The Mighty Quinn

## Mickey Quinn

*Leitrim for Croke Park. Mayo for Croagh Patrick.*
Sign outside a church in Leitrim after their Connacht title in 1994.

Gaelic football needs every nostalgic prop it can muster and when many of the controversies of today are forgotten the powerful grip Leitrim's Connacht final triumph exerted on the popular imagination will never vanish. In his radio commentary Micheál Ó Muircheartaigh said it was easy to imagine the Leitrim fans who had gone on to their eternal reward leaning over the bannisters in heaven watching the drama unfold. At the centre of that famous victory was Mickey Quinn who played under-age football for Leitrim for five years, twenty years for the senior team (1978–97) and nine years with the Over-40s. He made his senior inter-county debut in 1978. Although he was under 6 feet tall he could hold his own with giants like Liam McHale but his toughest battles were with Willie Joe Padden.

Leitrim football is not normally associated with the exotic but when Quinn first broke into the team he lined up with the county's closest ever equivalent to a David Beckham figure.

'We had a poor team at the time but we had a star in Mickey Martin. He was kind of a glamour boy but a great forward. Had he been with one of the footballing powers he would have been a household name but it was a case of "out of sight, out of mind".'

Glamour was alien to much of Quinn's own career.

'One day we were playing Mayo in Charlestown and there was such a gale blowing that, at one stage when the Mayo goalie kicked out the ball, it got caught in the wind and blew back over the inline for a forty-five.'

Throughout the 1980s Leitrim experienced nothing but disappointment.

'In 1983 Galway beat us by a point in injury time. I was sick the night before the All-Ireland final when Galway were preparing to meet Dublin in the final knowing we could have and should have beat them but we hadn't the confidence and lacked quality in the full-forward line.'

Things changed for the better for Quinn personally and Leitrim when P. J. Carroll became manager.

'We went on a fourteen or fifteen unbeaten game run which was very unusual for Leitrim and won an All-Ireland B final in 1990. I won an All-Star that year and as it was the first one in Leitrim, it caused a lot of excitement in the county and gave me a new lease of life even though I had two or three trips with them as replacements at that stage. It meant everything to me because it was always my burning ambition. Winning an All-Ireland with Leitrim was too much to hope for. We were playing Leinster in the 1984 Railway Cup in Ballinasloe when the journalist David Walsh told me that I had missed out on an All-Star the year before by just one vote.'

1994 was a memorable year for Leitrim. Their nearest neighbours had to be dealt with first.

'Roscommon had been the biggest bogey team for us. We had great battles with them in previous years but no matter what we threw at them they always seemed to have the upper hand. That spring, though, we relegated Roscommon from our division in the National League in Carrick-on-Shannon. We knew then we could beat them and we did in the Connacht Championship. In previous years we should have beat them but that year they should have beat us! We went on to take Mayo in the Connacht final. Although we made a dreadful start we had great belief and that was in large measure due to our manager.'

A major catalyst for Leitrim's taste of glory was the management of John O'Mahony. 'He is a very tough trainer. He took everybody back because he drove us so hard.

'There were evenings that we would turn up for training in Kells that would be so wet that you wouldn't let your dog out in it. We'd be wondering if he would send us out in the absolute deluge but he would be out just in a t-shirt and track-suit setting up the bollards. We'd be thinking: "This guy is off his rocker," but he was setting us an example. Then he stood in the corner and blew the whistle and we came out. There was always method to his madness. He brought us to train on the biggest sand dunes in Sligo and often there would be no hot showers afterwards but that toughened us up and then we were ready to move on to the next phase.

'One thing is attention to detail. He had music for us on the bus to games like Queen's "We Will Rock You". I remember the All-Ireland semi-final against Dublin in 1994. Every line on the pitch I looked at that day John had a water carrier, so that any time I wanted water I always had at least one in my vision.

'What it took for us to win a Connacht championship was massive. Winning an All-Ireland is nothing to Kerry because they are used to it but winning a Connacht title was a huge burden for us mentally because we had only ever won one and that back in 1927. John O'Mahony brought a psychologist on board, Frank Cogan. He started off by getting us to set goals. Then, before our first game, in his distinctive Scottish accent he asked what score we would concede. We said seven points. He asked: "Why not no goal and no point?" When we started to giggle he asked again: "Why not?" Each time we came up with a reason he came back and asked: "Why not?" Then when he asked us how much we would score we said: 2-10. He asked us: "Why not 7-24?" We all laughed and again he came back with: "Why not?" Then each time we offered a reason he again replied: "Why not?" Eventually we started to think why not? Then he split the defenders into one group, the forwards into another and got us to come up with our individual goals. The psychologist would then board the team bus about twenty minutes before we reached the ground on match days and that reinforced the messages he was putting across.

'John was brilliant at getting into the head of individual players. Colm McGlynn was a great full-forward for us but he always liked to think he was a bit special. He told John one night that he could not train one evening.

"Why?"

"I have exams in College. I can't train Thursday either."

"Why?"

"I have exams in College."

"Well, when are you free?"

"Ten o'clock on Wednesday night."

"OK, I will meet you in Ringsend at ten o'clock."

John travelled all the way to Dublin and ran the sh*t out of him. Colm never asked for special treatment again! That's the way John was. What he did for Leitrim was priceless.'

Leitrim were not to hit the same dizzy heights after 1994.

'Galway beat us by a point and then won the Connacht final by seventeen points. We should have beaten them. It was the biggest disappointment of my career. Some of our players were too cocky.'

From the outset Quinn and Declan Darcy had almost a mutual admiration society.

'Declan was playing in a Connacht trial and was marking Tomás Tierney. By that stage Tierney was a household name and Declan was just a whippersnapper nobody had heard of outside Leitrim. At one stage Declan

*Above:* Superquinn: Mickey Quinn soars in the air to win the ball for Leitrim in the 1994 All-Ireland semi-final against Dublin.

went into him like an express train and sent him sprawling. I said to him afterwards: "Did you know who you were doing that to?" I think, though, it showed everybody that reputations meant nothing to Declan and he was going to hold his own in any company.'

Aughawillian like Leitrim linked Darcy with Quinn. Quinn admits to playing a leading role in the infamous "battle of the fog".

'Aughawillian were playing Clann na Gael in the Connacht club championship but the match shouldn't have gone ahead. The fog was so bad you couldn't see the goalie kicking out the ball. Things heated up when two of our players were hit. I think it was me who really started it off! I "had a go" at Jimmy McManus and soon the whole set of players, subs and supporters were involved. The referee had a hard time getting law and order back but the game was a great battle in every sense.'

The match had an amusing postscript.

'Jerome Quinn played for Aughawillian against Clann na Gael that day and really dished it out to some of the Clann lads and developed a reputation as a hard nut. That was one of the reasons why Aughawillian versus Clann was renamed "the Provos versus the Guards". We were playing Roscommon in the Connacht Championship in 1990 and before the match our manager P. J. Carroll had an unusual mind game planned. He said: "Jerome Quinn, they all think you're f**king mad in Roscommon, what you need to do is pick up a clump of grass, stick it in your mouth and ate it in front of your marker's face. He'll sh*t himself." Jerome was wing-half-back and was marking a lovely, skilful player. Sure enough, Jerome did as he was told and you could see the Roscommon player's legs turn to jelly!'

Quinn picked a dream team of Connacht players.

1. Johnny Geraghty
(Galway)

2. Martin Carney   3. Seamus Quinn   4. Dermot Flanagan
(Mayo)   (Leitrim)   (Mayo)

5. Declan Meehan   6. Barnes Murphy   7. Declan Darcy
(Galway)   ( Sligo)   (Leitrim)

8. Dermot Earley   9. Willie Joe Padden
(Roscommon)   (Mayo)

10. Paddy Dolan   11. Seán Purcell   12. Mickey Martin
(Leitrim)   ( Galway)   (Leitrim)

13. Packy McGarty   14. Micheál Kearins   15. Tony McManus
(Leitrim)   (Sligo)   (Roscommon)

# The Conductor

## Kevin Walsh

Nobody in Galway bought more into John O'Mahony's ethos that champions take chances and pressure is a privilege than Kevin Walsh. It is O'Mahony's assessment rather than three All-Star awards which best captures Walsh's contribution to Galway's All-Ireland triumphs in 1998 and 2001.

'Padraig Joyce and Michael Donnellan rightly get a lot of credit for their roles in our success. Yet the man that orchestrated the whole show for us was Kevin Walsh. He was the guy who could see the moves and pulled the strings and won the ball for the forwards. Anybody who doubts his importance to the team need just look back to see the differences between our performances when he was missing like the defeat to Roscommon in 2001 and the way we played when he was there.'

Incredibly, at the age of thirteen Walsh had reached his full height of six foot four and like Liam McHale he initially made his mark in basketball, winning two Community Games titles and an All-Ireland Colleges title with St Paul's Oughterard. However, a dilemma soon presented itself. The bad knees that would haunt him throughout his career forced him to choose between basketball and Gaelic football. The choice became a lot easier when, in 1986, sixteen-year-old Walsh won an All-Ireland minor final. His brother Bosco played at corner-back during the same match.

The star of that team was John Joyce who looked set to become the next big thing in Gaelic football. It was not to be. Joyce was killed tragically in an accident in the Canary Islands.

In 1987 Walsh made his senior debut with Galway but injury quickly intervened and he did not establish himself as a Championship regular until the following year. Mayo, Roscommon and Leitrim were kingpins in Connacht until '95 when Walsh finally won a Connacht senior medal and a place in the All-Ireland semi-final against Peter Canavan's Tyrone.

'We missed three gilt edges to score in that game and that's what lost us the match. Gary Fahy held Peter really well though Canavan flicked a

*Above:* King Kevin: Kevin Walsh directs the show in the Galway midfield with regal authority despite the best efforts of Meath's Trevor Giles in the 2001 All-Ireland final. *Photo:* The Westmeath-Offaly Independent.

crucial goal. What I remember most from the game was the lack of support for us in Croke Park. I'd say there were only two-thousand Galway people in the stands. There was no real buzz. At the time, people felt that the standard was very bad in Connacht. Mayo changed that by going so close to winning the All-Ireland in 1996 and getting to the final again in 1997. It was clear that there were not many better teams in the country. When we beat Mayo in Castlebar in '98, I remember the incredible atmosphere and the reaction of the crowd as we came off the field. It was so different from '95. At that stage, we believed that something like an All-Ireland might be on. Roscommon brought the young players, who were taking things for granted in particular, back to reality when they drew with us in the Connacht final and pushed us all the way in the replay.'

Eventually the Galway team took heed of the O'Mahony mantra: take the opportunity of a lifetime in the lifetime of the opportunity. Walsh says, 'We were underdogs against Derry in the semi-final but beat them well. The hype in the county was incredible in the run-up to the All-Ireland but Johnno had been through it before with Mayo and he handled it well. He delegated two or three players to deal with the media which kept the press happy and kept the pressure off the younger players in particular. The first half did not go well for us and I'm sure a lot of Galway people felt we were in serious trouble. In the second half though we played more as an integrated unit and Ja Fallon had a serious ten minutes in the second half which set us on our way.

'It was an incredible atmosphere but I had got a kick in the calf fifteen minutes from the end and, while all the lads were jumping up and down, I collapsed on the ground. We had a huge sense of achievement especially as we were the first Connacht team to win an All-Ireland in thirty-two years. It was a real family occasion. My father, who has since passed on, was there in the stand. He was not a man to say much but I knew he was proud. My mother and my wife Mary were there also, as was our first child, Caoimhe, who was born that year.'

Contrary to the perception in certain quarters it was not partying that caused Galway to lose to Mayo in the Connacht Championship in 1999.

'The mentality of some of our players was very wrong on the day. Some fellas were trying to win the match on their own and didn't seem to realise that Mayo were still a good team. Three or four of our stars, especially in the forwards, could have and should have been taken off that day.'

In the Millennium Championship, injury forced Walsh to start on the bench for the All-Ireland final against Kerry. In the opening twenty-five minutes, Kerry completely outplayed Galway and led by 0-8 to 0-1. A less than fully fit Walsh was sprung and his value to the side was immediately seen as he took charge of midfield and Galway outscored Kerry by 0-6 to 0-2 in the closing ten minutes of the half. With the sides level and the final whistle in sight Derek Savage was given the chance to win the game for Galway but he did not take it. Walsh does not blame Savage for Galway's failure to win the game.

'The two big factors for us in 2000 were the back injury that lost us Tomás Mannion and the serious injury to Ja Fallon that threatened to destroy his career. I always believed that Ja was our best forward over the years. On his day Padraig Joyce could be the best footballer in the country like in the second half of the 2001 All-Ireland final but you never knew exactly what to expect from Padraig. In recent years, I feel that Padraig should not be deployed at full-forward but in the half-forward line. What the team needed was someone who would break the ball to bring Michael Meehan and the other corner-forward into the play. Liam Sammon made that change in 2008. Ja was a better link player and more consistent than our other forwards.'

While Walsh played a significant part in the replay while he was on the pitch, injury caused him to miss most of it. Without his hand at the wheel, Galway floundered and lost the match.

'There was still a feeling that there was another All-Ireland in the team but losing to Roscommon in the Connacht Championship in 2001 came as a shock. A lot of surgery was done on the team afterwards and it was needed. Wicklow were a potential banana skin for us in the qualifiers. To be honest, we were scared going down there because we weren't sure of our own form and people spoke of the "boot of the car factor" [famously, a referee had been locked in the boot of a car after a game] in Aughrim and that Wicklow were always hard to beat. We won but, to be candid, we were lucky not to have faced a stronger team because I don't think we would have been able for a good team at that stage. To win, though, was a huge thing for us. After the defeat against Roscommon, we had a lot of soul searching to do. Fellas were hurt because of what had happened in '99 and in the previous year, and we started to get our heads right and then we went on a roll to get to the All-Ireland. Meath hammered Kerry in the other semi-final and Johnno was brilliant at talking down our chances in the media, which kept all the pressure off us as Meath were red-hot favourites.

'I was never as confident about winning a match as going into that game. Twelve of that Meath team had played in '96 and Mayo should have beaten them. I knew they were not as good as people thought they were. In the first half we had so much ball but we weren't using it in the forward line

*Above:* The eagle has landed: Giant Galway midfielder Kevin Walsh goes highest for the ball in an aerial duel during the 1998 All-Ireland final victory over Kildare. *Photo:* Irish Examiner/*Denis Minihane*

and went in level. After the defeats of the previous years, the forwards seemed to be lacking in confidence. At half-time, the one point I made was that if the forwards had got so much ball in training they would have dusted our backs. In the second half, they did cut loose and we won by nine points.

'People talk about how great it is to beat Kerry in the All-Ireland. The one team I always wanted to beat in a final was Meath. They had won two titles in the '80s and the '90s. I was sick listening to Colm O'Rourke on the television going on about how great his Meath team were.'

As Galway were unable to emulate such success in the next years there was a lot of speculation about disharmony in the camp. Such talk was accentuated when, in his post-match interview on RTÉ television after Galway lost to Kerry in 2002, Padraig Joyce appeared to suggest that it was time for John O'Mahony to consider stepping down as manager. Walsh is emphatic in his dismissal of this chatter.

'There was a huge rumour in 1999 that Ray Silke had a huge bust-up with the Donnellan brothers. There was never a word between them. There was no animosity in the camp whatsoever. The reason we went downhill had a lot to do with diminished hunger. One factor that is often forgotten is that Niall Finnegan was a huge loss to us when he retired so young. He always stood up to the plate for us.'

Injuries and the demands of a young family caused Walsh to quit the game in 2004. When his kids are older he would like to take on a coaching role at some stage. He left the scene with some amusing memories.

'We were away on a team holiday and Seán O'Domhnaill was messing and pulled down the togs of let's say a prominent county board official in full view of everyone. Needless to say the man in question was not too happy. Later, when Seán was sunbathing on the beach the official sneaked up and took the wallet which was lying beside him. When he figured out what was happening Seán ran after him down the beach. They were not a physical match and Seán was catching up with him so your man threw the wallet into the ocean. He couldn't understand when Seán started laughing. The wallet belonged to Ja Fallon's wife and she asked Seán to mind it while she went for a swim!'

Walsh's dream team is:

1. John O'Leary
(Dublin)

2. Seán Marty Lockhart     3. Darren Fay      4. Tomás Mannion
(Derry)                    (Meath)            (Galway)

5. Martin O'Connell     6. Seamus Moynihan      7. Seán Óg de Paor
(Meath)                 (Kerry)                 (Galway)

8. Jack O'Shea                    9. Liam McHale
(Kerry)                          (Mayo)

10. Ja Fallon      11. Larry Tompkins      12. Maurice Fitzgerald
(Galway)           (Cork)                  (Kerry)

13. Colm 'Gooch' Cooper   14. Peter Canavan      15. Mickey Linden
(Kerry)                   (Tyrone)               (Down)

# The Tourlestrane Talisman

## Eamonn O'Hara

The ultimate test of a player in any sport is that they have the power to make the pulse skip a beat whenever they are in full flight. Once they get the ball, a buzz of expectancy goes around the ground. For an entire generation, the defining image of Sligo football has been the penetrating runs of Eamonn O'Hara. In full flight, he lights up the pitch like a flash of forked lightning, flashing brilliantly, thrilling and, from the opposition's point of view, frightening.

In 2007, he produced the defining image of the football championship in the Connacht final against Galway. He took a pass from David Kelly fifty yards from the Galway goal. With the defence trailing desperately in his wake, he made over 30 yards before unleashing a rocket of a shot to the roof of the net. A thirty-two-year famine had come to an end for Sligo.

'We said before the game, it's not about heroes today, it's not about a fella getting ten or twelve points on the board or about personal vendettas. It's all about working as hard for the Sligo team, putting your neck on the line; fellas did that and it's what it took. We hadn't done that completely in thirty-two years.'

O'Hara first played senior football for Sligo in 1993 in a challenge match against Mayo when he was just seventeen years old and found himself marking the vastly experienced John Finn. The low point of his career came the following year.

'I was playing against Mayo in the Connacht Championship in midfield and thought that I was doing OK but I was substituted after twenty minutes. Somebody had to be a scapegoat and I was the choice. The management probably thought that they were protecting me but it was a long, lonely walk off the pitch. I learned from it, though, and promised that I would never let myself down again by ever having to be taken off in a match.'

At the time, playing for Sligo had very little glamour. 'We were playing in front of small crowds and in not very glamorous venues. I suppose the best illustration of it was when we went down to play Kilkenny in a

League match. When we got off the bus there were seven or eight thousand people there and we thought that was great. What we hadn't realised was that the Kilkenny hurlers were playing first and by the time we ran on to the pitch there were about two people in the stand.'

The arrival of Mickey Moran was a catalyst in the upturn in the county's fortunes.

'We started to do well in the League in '97, '98 and '99. We beat Kerry in the League in '97 in Kerry and we also beat Dublin in Markievicz Park, which was great. We were always capable of creating a shock. The bigger the team the more we liked it and the better we played.'

2000 was a turning point for O'Hara and the team as a whole. 'We beat Mayo in the Connacht Championship by three points in Markievicz Park. It was a huge relief to finally beat one of the big teams in Connacht. We kind of lost the run of ourselves before playing Galway in the Connacht semi-final, thinking we were about to make a breakthrough. Galway were on fire that day and we failed to get a single score in the first half. Everything they tried, even the most outlandish, came off. Niall Finnegan got a point from such an acute angle that it defied the laws of physics. We lost the game in the end by eighteen points. A lot of fingers were pointed at me after the game. I learned a valuable lesson that day though. After the game against Mayo I had been treated like a hero so I discovered that there's only six inches between a pat on the back and a kick in the ass.'

Criticism is not something that bothers O'Hara unduly though his intense will to win does not always endear him to some, who confuse it with arrogance. His lack of interest in playing in the Tommy Murphy Cup may not be popular with the GAA authorities but reflects his disinterest in being second best.

'People are very quick to judge you. The odd time you might hear people talking about you and saying: "He's a right f**ker." I'm not there to entertain people and I am the way I am and if people don't like me it doesn't bother me. I keep my head straight through talking with friends and through getting away from the hustle and bustle on the family farm.'

A summer in Chicago playing with St Brendan's refreshed O'Hara and his return coincided with Peter Ford's arrival as Sligo manager.

'Peter brought that arrogance that Sligo had never had before and his attitude, his level of preparation and his organisation were eye-openers to us all. Sometimes he trained with us and he wouldn't ask us to do anything that he wouldn't do himself. We did really well in a lot of games in the qualifiers. Beating Kildare in a thriller in Croke Park was the start of it. Looking back now, while those wins – like defeating Tyrone – were great, we

*Above:* Get your hand off: Eamonn O'Hara receives close attention from Roscommon in the never-to-be-forgotten 2007 Connacht Championship.
*Photo:* The Sligo Champion/*Leo Gray*

won nothing. While we played well at times we have nothing to show for it. We had the beating of Armagh in both games but we missed vital chances. I suppose for most people it was story of "should have beens" and "what ifs" and people say we should have got a penalty. In fact, what happened was that I was one of four players to miss scoring chances and that's what cost us the game. Most Sligo people saw it as a good year because we reached an All-Ireland quarter-final but when I saw Kieran McGeeney lifting the Sam Maguire Cup six weeks after they beat us I was thinking it was a bad year because we had won nothing.'

From a personal point of view the year saw O'Hara become the third Sligo player to win an All-Star award. His achievement was lavishly celebrated within the county but the team's fortunes went into decline.

'Things went down a bit in 2003. Peter probably stayed on a year too long and a few lads opted out or retired. We had to rebuild and bring in some new faces. We did OK in the league and maintained our Division One status but the next few years were lean ones.' Managers came and went, most controversially Dom Corrigan. 'He was a very nice guy but he was brought in to get results and they didn't come. Things were disjointed around then as well because some players decided to play in the Tommy Murphy Cup, some of us didn't, realising it's complete bullshi*t and people weren't on the same wavelength. But the way it ended was blown out of all proportion like it was from the Mafia or something. There was no white van, no players locked in the dressing room. Dom was normally there for training at seven, got delayed, rolled in the gate and the county board guys were waiting to have a quiet chat.'

O'Hara has been described as Gaelic football's answer to Chuck Norris. He had the opportunity to showcase his competitive spirit to the nation when he played for Ireland in the Compromise Rules.

'I had been doing the training sessions for a number of years but was cut from the final panel when Colm O'Rourke was in charge which surprised a lot of people. I think Colm had his mind made up before the trial games but he won the series and you can't argue with success. When Brian McEniff took charge though I was selected and going to Australia was the experience of a lifetime. We won the series which was great, though, losing at home the next year – especially with the violence that marred the spectacle – was a disappointment.'

O'Hara used the whole International Rules as a personal research project. 'I was mixing and sharing rooms with players who had won All-Irelands or experienced great success. I saw myself as a messenger who would relay what I learned to the Sligo team. The big players on the Irish team were all winners. In Sligo we went out to play games in hope. These guys went out in expectation. Our mentality was that we were happy with a good performance. This attitude came from the County Board, from managers, from the general public and from friends and did seep into our consciousness, which led to: "Ah well, sure, we never expected too much" syndrome. It was because of our attitude that we had never been good enough to win anything. What was different about Sligo in 2007 was that our attitude was no longer about doing well but about winning and doing whatever it took to get a title at last.'

O'Hara plays down the significance of his stunning goal in the Connacht final.

'If we had taken all the chances we had in the game my goal would have had no importance. It was not about me. It was about winning the Nestor Cup at last.'

He has no fixed plans about the future. 'I hope to play on for a few years yet. I believe if you are free from injury, that if your head is right, your body will be right. I will know when it's time to go if a young fella is outpacing me. I've been asked to do bits in the media and if opportunities came my way and they suited me, I wouldn't mind some more of it. When I hang up my football boots I'd love to go into another sport like doing a triathlon or a marathon.'

O'Hara's appeal is international. 'I got a text from friends on holiday in Portugal. They were surprised to see a Portuguese boy approaching wearing a Sligo jersey. When they turned around the saw the number eight on his back with the word "O'Hara"!'

Although at the time it was not funny, O'Hara now laughs at a case of mistaken identity.

'We were playing Westmeath in 2006. I was given a second yellow card for a foul even though I was forty yards away at the time. The linesman fingered me because he mistook me for Seán Davey because we have the same colour. I'm naturally like this. Seán gets his colouring from a sunbed. It was farcical more anything else.'

O'Hara's dream team is:

1. Declan O'Keeffe
(Kerry)

2. Marc Ó Sé  3. Darren Fay  4. Seán Marty Lockhart
(Kerry)  (Meath)  (Derry)

5. Seán Óg de Paor  6. Seamus Moynihan  7. Anthony Rainbow
(Galway)  (Kerry)  (Kildare)

8. Darragh Ó Sé  9. Anthony Tohill
(Kerry)  (Derry)

10. Ja Fallon  11. Trevor Giles  12. Michael Donnellan
(Galway)  (Meath)  (Galway)

13. Peter Canavan  14. Padraig Joyce  15. Maurice Fitzgerald
(Tyrone)  (Galway)  (Kerry)

Fast Forward

# The Terrible Twin

## Frank Stockwell

The late Jack Mahon was well able to tell stories against himself. He once bumped into a young man in Galway and was a bit disappointed to hear that the youngster had never heard of him. He hoped he might impress his new acquaintance when he told him that he played at centre-half-back on the Galway team that beat Cork in the 1956 All-Ireland final.

'Gosh, that's shocking,' said the youngster.

*Preceding page:* Goalbound: Joe Young (left) watches as Galway launch an attack on the Cork goal in the 1956 All-Ireland final, with Frank Stockwell (third from left) lurking ominously in mid-air. Cork's Pádraig Tyers (fourth from left) does his best to stop the ball while Donal O'Sullivan and Paddy Harrington run in from the right.

*Below:* Watch him: Pádraig Tyers in the Cork defence keeps a close watch on Frank Stockwell in the 1956 All-Ireland final, closely followed by Cork defenders Mick Gould and Donal O'Sullivan. Dan Murray brings up the rear on the far right. Note the umpire smoking during the match – a sure sign of the times.

'Why?' asked a bemused Jack.

'Because I've just discovered my dad's a liar. He's always said that when Galway won that All-Ireland, they never had a centre-back!'

That 1956 final turned Frank Stockwell into one of the GAA immortals. The late RTÉ Gaelic Games Correspondent, Mick Dunne coined the phrase 'the terrible twins' to describe Seán Purcell's unique partnership with Frank Stockwell. He explained the origin of the phrase to me.

'Galway's Seán Purcell was the best player I ever saw. It could be said that there were better players in different positions but as far as I'm concerned he was the best all-round footballer. I remember him at full-back in the Connacht semi-final in 1954 against Mayo. It was one of the finest individual displays I've ever seen. He played on the great Tom Langan, then Danny Neill and then John Nallen, but it was all the same, Purcell was superb. He was also a magnificent midfielder and he was the brains of the Galway team that won the All-Ireland in 1956 at centre-forward. He had such a wonderful combination with the other Galway maestro, Frankie Stockwell, and they performed such a lethal duo that I described them as the "terrible twins" and, to my pleasant surprise, the phrase entered the GAA vernacular about them.'

*Centre:* Hero of the hour: Frank Stockwell is carried off the pitch after scoring 2-5 in the 1956 All-Ireland final against Cork.
*Right:* Frankly speaking: (from left) Frank Stockwell and Sean Purcell chase the ball with Cork's Denis Bernard and Dan Murray in the 1956 All-Ireland final.

The words of Katy Dobey's poem probably best sum up their unique relationship:

We were like two stones side by side on a sandy beach:
We touched accidentally, but we touched forever.
Joint somewhere deep beneath the surface
In a friendship that's eternal.

Seán Purcell reserved special place for Stockwell. 'We were known as the terrible twins because we had such a great understanding and because we did a lot of damage to opposing defences. Frank was a fabulous footballer. The fact that he scored 2-5 in the 1956 All-Ireland final speaks for itself. They were all off his foot, no frees. He destroyed the Cork defence on his own. It was just a matter of getting the ball in to him the best way we could. We tried the old tricks we had worked on over the years. Things were much less scientific, I suppose, than they are now. We all contributed to each other but we all knew Frank was the man to give the ball to and he'd do the rest. You have to remember that was a sixty-minute final. I'm great friends with Jimmy Keaveney but when he broke Frank's record by scoring 2-6 in the 1977 All-Ireland final he had a seventy-minute game to do it in.

'It's a simple game really. If you give the ball to somebody, the best way that he can get it is if you don't pass when he has two or three men marking him. You give it to him so that he can run and move to get it himself. Frank would know that you were going to put the ball in a particular place. He would sense that. There was nothing made up about it. It was natural skill on Frank's part. We'd a natural sort of empathy with each other and it worked out well. We managed to click together. There was nothing too organised about it. We just took it naturally.

'I always tried to get the ball and part with it to the best of my ability, whether to score or to give it to somebody in a better position. I suppose I was lucky to have a good sense of anticipation. I remember when I was a young lad in the college we used to have a couple of hours free after school and we'd be kicking the ball around. There would be a great crowd out on the field and you had to be very lucky or very good to get a kick at the ball. It would certainly improve your anticipation. You'd nearly know where everybody was going to kick it. You had to if you were going to get a kick at it yourself.

'Frank would have been a brilliant soccer player. He knew the simple things of the game, especially how to pass. I'd give it to him, and he'd give it back to me or vice versa. We knew how to pass the ball to one another, and give each other the old one-twos. I'd give it to him so that he could move to get it and sometimes he would give me the ball back. We knew each other's play and wherever we might be we could find each other easy enough. 'Twas a natural knowledge of each other's strengths and weaknesses. In that way, we managed to put up the scores.'

Enda Colleran also had great affection for Stockwell.

'From the dawn of time identification with heroes has been an integral part of the human condition. Great sporting performances have always grabbed the imagination of the young of all ages as they fantasise about emulating the glorious feats of their heroes. The most casual of Galway fans took vicarious pride in the style, craft, courage and character that fired our imagination when Galway won the All-Ireland in 1956 and because Frank scored 2-5 in the final I think young fellas like me had a special identification with him.

'Football left him with a wealth of happy memories. He once told me about one of his first club games as a minor. At that stage, it was hard to field a team. There was one guy roped into play for them and he was provided with boots, socks, a jersey and the lot. They were thrashed and, of course, when that happens everybody blames everybody else. When unflattering comments were put to the new recruit, his riposte was, "Well, you can't blame me. I never got near the ball!"

'Frank has a great feeling for Galway and the West was particularly proud that four Connacht players were chosen on the Centenary team of the century.'

That team was:

1. Danno Keeffe
(Kerry)

2. Enda Colleran        3. Paddy O'Brien        4. Seán Flanagan
(Galway)                   (Meath)                      (Mayo)

5. Seán Murphy         6. John Joe Reilly        7. Stephen White
(Kerry)                     (Cavan)                       (Louth)

8. Mick O'Connell                    9. Jack O'Shea
(Kerry)                                   (Kerry)

10. Seán O'Neill        11. Seán Purcell        12. Pat Spillane
(Down)                     (Galway)                    (Kerry)

13. Mike Sheehy        14. Tom Langan        15. Kevin Heffernan
(Kerry)                     (Mayo)                       (Dublin)

# The Green and Red of Mayo

## Willie McGee

Former Detective Superintendent Willie McGee of the Garda Fraud Squad cuts an imposing figure. His many talents as a player were publicly acknowledged when he was nominated as one of the ten top full-forwards for a place on the Team of the Century in 1984. The position, in fact, went to another Mayo man, Tom Langan, but the nomination was nonetheless 'a great honour'. McGee was subsequently picked on the Centenary team of greatest players who never won an All-Ireland. When he heard the news he thought it was a prank, and candidly admits, 'I didn't expect to be selected.'

The Burrishoole goal-scoring supremo announced his arrival on the national stage in bold print when he scored four golden goals in the All-Ireland Under-21 football final repay of 1967. Only the great Mike Sheehy was able to take his title as the most prolific goal-scorer in the history of Gaelic football. The high point of his career came in the National League final against Down in 1970.

'I had three stitches in my eye – I accidentally bumped into a fella in a soccer game and I can't recall all that much of it. We were all so excited about winning, maybe that blurred the memory. The one thing I remember from the match is John Gibbons sending in a high ball. I was standing in front of the goalkeeper and I went to catch it, sold a dummy in the air, and the ball went straight into the net. The thing was, I never got any credit for it. I can't repeat what the goalie said to me!

'We thought that was the start of a great new chapter in Mayo's history. It was the first success we had in years and we got carried away. Mayo always had a big problem coping with being favourites and never lost it! I think, too, that Mayo's style of football is that they go out to please rather than to win. They never had that "win at all cost" bred into them.'

He captained Mayo in 1975 but an injury sustained in a basketball match the following year ended McGee's career.

'I got back to fitness after three operations on my ankle. I made myself available to the county after playing a representative game in the

*Above:* Man and ball: Willie McGee bundles the ball into the net in unorthodox fashion to score a goal for Mayo in a League fixture in 1969.

Gardaí against the Universities, when I scored 1-4 on the Kildare full-back, Paddy O'Donoghue. I had everything to lose by going back. People like Mick O'Dwyer, Mick O'Connell and Paddy McCormack had done so without great success. You were on a hiding to nothing if you came out of retirement and your side still lost. I was fitter than when I had been playing; I had finally realised the importance of training hard, and I was training like I never trained before. But I was married and had a mortgage and I was a garda who often had to work on Sundays, so it was just a question of being paid a proper allowance. Unfortunately, we didn't come to an agreement on that.'

It was not McGee's first brush with GAA officialdom in Mayo. 'I got into trouble with the County Board about playing in New York without getting permission, and they suspended me. I told the County Board chairman I was just ignorant of the rules. He told me to put it in writing but I answered back that that they hadn't put it in writing when they suspended me, and if word of mouth was good enough for them it ought to be good enough for me! There was a stand-off position for a while and then, one day I was on duty in Grafton Street when a priest, Fr Paddy Mahon, met me. He followed me up and down the beat for an hour in order to persuade me to change my mind. Eventually I relented. I wrote my piece to the County Board on the back of a cigarette box.

'A short while later I had occasion to go to England for work reasons. I was seen in the airport heading for departures at the same time as a plane to America was called, and I was reported to the County Board. I was duly asked if I was playing in New York. Given my previous experience, I told them to come back to me when they had evidence. I didn't make them any the wiser whether I had played Gaelic football or not.'

McGee had reason to be worried about being reported on another occasion. 'When I first started playing championship football the ban was still in operation, so you daren't be seen at a soccer or rugby match, or play them either. I vividly remember attending a soccer match in Dalymount Park one day when I heard this chant, "Burrishoole, Burrishoole!" coming from behind the goal. I lifted my collar up to hide my face because I was scared stiff of being reported, but it was a Roscommon man and good friend of mine, Noel Carthy. I was glad to know it was him!'

Since his retirement, McGee has been disappointed by the level of aggression that sometimes mars the game.

'Because teams train more they're probably more likely to wade in and defend their colleague, which sometimes leads to a free-for-all. There is also a lot of pressure on managers to win, which is fuelled by the media. We have a situation that, for a successful manager, there can be handsome rewards. Let's be honest about it, a successful manager can make a lot of money nowadays, so that adds to the pressure.'

When Mayo football seemed to be in disarray during the former Dublin player Brian McDonald's controversial tenure as county trainer, McGee was recruited in a campaign to take corrective action.

'I felt at the time that Jack O'Shea was the man to bring some good days back to the county. Some people close to the top in Mayo football had the same view and I was asked by the chairman of the County Board, Christy Loftus, to raise the funds from the friends of Mayo in Dublin and to personally approach Jacko to take on the Mayo job. To be fair to him, I think that given the travel involved he deserved to be properly looked after. Things didn't work out the way people hoped, however, as again we raised the funds to be able to offer the post to John Maughan.'

McGee was involved for a time in training some of Mayo's Dublin-based county players, such as Liam McHale and Anthony 'Fat Larry' Finnerty, who was one of the great characters of Mayo football. He was fat in the winter but lost a lot of weight in the summer. Some years later during a training session with Brian McDonald, Finnerty was one of twenty-three

*Left:* Ebony and Ivory: Willie McGee shares a tender moment with a young friend at a community relations event in Dublin's inner city in 1994

or twenty-four players who were jogging around the pitch. McDonald told them that everytime he blew his whistle, they were to jump high in the air and imagine they were catching a famous ball. This drill went on until they got level with the dressing room when Finnerty started to zoom towards the dressing room. The irate trainer shouted at him, 'Where are you going?' Fat Larry replied, 'I'm just going in to get my gloves. That blady ball you want us to catch is awful slippy!'

Once some of the Mayo team went to the Cheltenham festival and heard a racket from one of the tents. They went in to investigate only to see Anthony having a crawling race with somebody else to great hilarity.

McGee's dream team is as follows:

1. Johnny Geraghty
(Galway)

| 2. Johnny Carey | 3. Noel Tierney | 4. Paddy McCormack |
|:---:|:---:|:---:|
| (Mayo) | (Galway) | (Offaly) |
| 5. John Donnellan | 6. John Morley | 7. Gerry O'Malley |
| (Galway) | (Mayo) | (Roscommon) |

8. Mick O'Connell          9. Dermot Earley
(Kerry)                    (Roscommon)

| 10. Packy McGarty | 11. Pat Griffin | 12. Micheál Kearins |
|:---:|:---:|:---:|
| (Leitrim) | (Kerry) | (Sligo) |
| 13. John Egan | 14. Seán O'Neill | 15. Jimmy Keaveney |
| (Kerry) | (Down) | (Dublin) |

# The Winner Takes It All

## Martin Carney

Martin Carney's senior inter-county career lasted twenty years. He came to national prominence when he was part of the Donegal team that won the county's first Ulster title in 1972. He also played his part when Donegal won a second provincial title in 1974. Crucial to Donegal's breakthrough was Brian McEniff.

'I know Brian as a friend and as a club mate. He didn't understand anything other than trying to win. His ambition to succeed was not part of the Donegal psyche to that point. John Tobin's career as a player is probably defined by the disappointment of the 1974 All-Ireland defeat to Dublin. Yet when we played Galway in the All-Ireland semi-final that year John led us on a merry dance. He was a gifted player with an amazing body swerve. People often forget that those games lasted eighty minutes and were very severe on the body. I was playing in midfield that year and I know!'

Carney's strong family ties led him to transfer to the green and red of Mayo in 1979.

'The best place to know where you are from is to visit graveyards and see how many names you recognise. I loved playing for Donegal and that is where I am from but things were not going well for Donegal and we were destroyed by Derry in 1978. Good work was being done at underage level, which reaped a reward years later but basically, we were a mess at that stage.

'My father is a Mayo man and my uncle, Jackie Carney, trained Mayo to win the All-Ireland final in both 1950 and '51, having played on the Mayo team that won the All-Ireland in 1936. I was teaching there then and I've always been happy there. The first couple of years saw us losing to Roscommon in the Connacht championship but we had a good run in the League in '81 and then suckered Galway, the National League champions, to win the Connacht final. Kerry were at their best that year. We kept up with them for an hour in the All-Ireland semi-final but we had nothing to match them after that. On a personal level, it was nice to captain the team but I think its real value was to re-establish a little bit of worth to Mayo football, not having won a Connacht title in the 1970s.'

Although Galway crushed Mayo the following year in the Connacht final, the game produced some moments of theatre as a by-election was taking place in Galway at a time. This was the year of GUBU and the Fianna Fáil government did not have an overall majority, and the outcome was very important.

'Charlie Haughey and half the cabinet were there. There were helicopters landing in the stadium, which was unheard of at the time in a GAA match. It was more like the Epsom Derby than a Connacht final.'

After the hiding in the Connacht final Carney credits two men with Mayo's revival. 'Liam O'Neill took over as manager and he was succeeded by John O'Mahony. They were very contrasting personalities and could never have worked together but what Liam put in place, John built on. Initially, though, Liam was to benefit from John's work with the Under-21 All-Ireland winning side in 1983 in the form of a number of new players. We won a Connacht title in '85 and found ourselves playing Dublin in the All-Ireland semi-final and then the replay. It was thrilling stuff and there was a real buzz in playing Dublin, with all the noisy atmosphere and theatre they bring. If we had played Kerry there would have been none of that because Kerry don't travel to All-Ireland semi-finals. We could have won the drawn game but they were that bit steadier in the second game. I am not doing an Arsene Wenger but I didn't see what happened to John Finn but he was a real mess in the dressing room at half-time in the first game. It was a testament to his stubbornness that he went out and played in the second half though I wonder how he was let out to play when he clearly wasn't fit.'

In 1988 Mayo were back in an All-Ireland semi-final, eventually losing to Meath.

'I loved playing Meath. They were a fierce, manly and honest team though if it was needed they would rearrange your features!

'This time, though, things were a bit different. Up to then, Mayo had always been a rollercoaster, from one extreme to the other. We were either fully up or completely down but John O'Mahony kept things grounded. We won the Connacht title again in 1989, when Liam McHale literally owned the ball and gave one of the great individual displays. We also had Seán Maher in the side, who was a very under-rated player and he gave us that enforcer rather than a creator presence we badly needed. Anthony Finnerty famously described Jimmy Burke's goal that year as "the push-over goal". It kind of bounced off him.

'For a county that had not won an All-Ireland final for so long, there was such an outpouring of goodwill and an incredible longing to win. Johnno tried to control it as best he could but a lot of local interests were looking for a slice of the action. When we scored the goal, I can recall looking down the Cork bench and seeing the sense of shock. They were as brittle as us in a different way but John Cleary and Michael McCarthy took over and they deservedly won. Although we lost, the team was feted and there was plenty of back-slapping that created its own problems and the team was distracted the next year and the opportunity to build on the advances of 1989 was lost.'

Why did Mayo fail to win an All-Ireland since 1951?

'I can't answer that. Part of it was that for a long time we were too nice and could get bullied, though that changed since John Maughan's time. History and emigration were also contributory factors.'

Although best known in recent years as a pundit on RTÉ television and Today FM, Carney is also involved in John O'Mahony's back-up team in Mayo, with responsibility for 'stats'. What is the secret of O'Mahony's success?

'He is very loyal and trusts people and expects the same in return. His man-management skills were probably best shown in Galway in the way he got a lot out of players, especially those that might have been seen as a little difficult like Michael Donnellan. Likewise in Mayo he handled Padraig Brogan well in all the circumstances. He could convince the likes of Seán Maher that he was a peerless midfielder, although that would not have been the popular belief in Mayo, but Seán had a massive influence. He is also extremely organised and has a finger in every aspect of the organisation and he is prepared to leave no stone unturned. He is also a good human being.'

As a member of the Football Development Committee, Carney was one of the instigators of the new Championship structure.

'We provided a badly needed facelift for the Championship with the qualifier system. At the moment, I think the area needs to be revisited again because the club is losing out too much. I think, though, we increased the profile of the game.'

Carney also had a stint as selector on the Compromise Rules team which saw him tour to Australia with the Irish team in 2003. One player made a strong impression on him.

'Kieran McGeeney was a great leader. I was very taken by him because he was the guy who would get things to happen and he raised the standard for others.'

*Above:* Turning-point: Martin Carney glides out of trouble to set up another attack for Mayo during the All-Ireland semi-final replay against Dublin in 1985.

Carney had a keen appreciation of a number of players from his own era.

'The hero of my first ever Croke Park game was Mick O'Connell and I remember meeting him for the first time in Galway as a student. Mick was doing a Sea Skipper course in Galway and my friend Tony "The Horse" Regan was asked to find a couple of fellas to train with Mick out in Pearse Stadium and I was one of the chosen few. We climbed in over the wall and I remember Micko running around the stadium in a pair of sawn-off wellingtons. He took off the wellies and put on the football boots and we had a fine training session together.

'I only won one Railway Cup medal with the Combined Universities in 1973. I played for Ulster in 1975 and remember it as Seán O'Neill's last game for Ulster. Jimmy Barry-Murphy scored 4-1 in that game from five kicks of the ball. Jimmy had played the day before in a Senior Hurling Club final for the 'Barrs against Johnstown and I remember meeting him that night and, let's put it this way, he was enjoying himself!'

Carney has another strong memory of a Railway Cup match.

'I was playing corner-back for Connacht against Leinster in Ballinasloe and marking Johnny Mooney and the first ball that went in Johnny got a goal. Afterwards, I couldn't understand why a section of the crowd was giving me terrible abuse and that continued for the rest of the game. I found out later that they were patients from the local psychiatric hospital who were let out for the day!'

His dream team is:

1. Billy Morgan
(Cork)

2. Robbie O'Malley     3. Mick Lyons     4. Paudie Lynch
(Meath)               (Meath)             (Kerry)

5. Páidí Ó Sé     6. Kieran McGeeney     7. Martin O'Connell
(Kerry)            (Armagh)           (Meath)

8. Jack O'Shea           9. Brian Mullins
(Kerry)                (Dublin)

10. Michael Donnellan     11. Brian McGuigan     12. Pat Spillane
(Galway)             (Tyrone)            (Kerry)

13. Mike Sheehy     14. Peter Canavan     15. Matt Connor
(Kerry)            (Tyrone)           (Offaly)

# Super Trooper

## Kevin McStay

Kevin McStay is happy to be known today as the guy who talks and writes about football rather than as a man who used to play the game. His career as a pundit on The Sunday Game came about almost by accident.

'I had broken my leg again in 1990 and was missing too much time from work. I was beginning to lose my appetite so I retired from the game. I was talking to one of my army colleagues in Athlone, Christy Rock – we call him Dickie Rock! – about the level of analysis on TV and he said: "You should do it!" Acting out of character, I wrote to Michael Lyster because his family and mine have family connections and a month later I got a call asking me to come for a trial run one evening on The Monday Game and it took off from there. That was over ten years ago and I really enjoy it.'

Into every pundit's life, some rain must fall. McStay is keenly aware of the moral of the GAA analyst, the donkey and the bridge: a man and his son were bringing their donkey to the fair. The man was walking with the donkey and his son was up on the animal's back. A passer-by said, 'Isn't it a disgrace to see that poor man walking and the young fella up on the donkey having an easy time? He should walk and let his poor father have a rest.'

So the boy dismounted and the father took his place. A mile later, they met another man who said: 'Isn't it a disgrace to have that boy walking while his father takes it easy? You should both get up on the donkey's back.'

They duly did but a short time later they met an enraged woman who screamed, 'How cruel it is to have two healthy men up on that poor donkey's back? The two of you should get down and carry the donkey.' Again they did as they were told but as they walked over the bridge, the donkey fell into the river and drowned.

The moral is that if you are an analyst and you are trying to please everyone you might as well kiss your ass goodbye.

'Modern punditry is much tighter than it was twenty years ago. I knew going into the job that there would be hard days when you would annoy or hurt people with your comments. There were times when it was not easy to say the tough things I did about Mayo players. I am there, though, to do a job and I try and live by the same rules as I do in my life in general. Am I willing to tell the truth as I see it? Am I willing to be corrected? I am well aware that families and friends of players see things through different spectacles when you are talking about their loved ones, just as my family thought I never played a bad game but you have to call it as you see it and sometimes that will generate controversy and you get lots of angry emails and letters and there are times when you get eyeballed by people which is not very comfortable.'

A Mayo exile living in Roscommon town, McStay has coached the Roscommon minors and Roscommon Gaels as well as Mayo's Under-21s. He has drawn on his experiences as a pundit in his coaching career.

'One thing you learn from the calls and texts to The Sunday Game is that everybody thinks they're a referee. One of the first things I do when I take over a team is give everybody thirty questions on the rules of the game. Most players get five or six right. Then I tell them that I don't want to see any of them whining to referees because a ref would have got twenty-nine out of thirty in the test and they are not to be wasting time and energy complaining when they don't know the rules themselves.'

In his professional life, McStay's job brings great variety. In April 2008, he completed a tour of duty with the 37th Irish Infantry Group on a peacekeeping mission to Kosovo.

'I was Group Logistics Officer so I had to take responsibility for sourcing anything from a tank to a towel. Essentially, my job was to be in charge of accomodation, food and transport for one-hundred-and-eighty army personnel. Anything can crop up so you've got to be very organised and, if possible, keep very calm. It is a great adventure but the hard part

*Below:* McStaying Power: Kevin McStay on the lookout while on army duty in Kosovo in 2008.

about an overseas duty is being away from your family.'

1983 was an exciting year for McStay's footballing development but it was not without pain.

'My very first senior game for Mayo was in the Connacht final in 1983 and I was marking the great Johnny Hughes. Although we were badly beaten that day, we were flying with the Under-21s and raced all the way to the All-Ireland final with a series of big wins though we drew the All-Ireland final against Derry in a game we should have won. I broke my ankle earlier in the summer and only came on as a sub in the second half. The replay was in Irvinestown and it was the first All-Ireland to be played in the north. It was great to win it and almost all of that team went on to play senior for Mayo at some stage and many of us went on to backbone the team that contested the All-Ireland final in 1989.'

In 1985, McStay hit the form of his life, winning an All-Star, as Mayo took Dublin to a replay in the All-Ireland semi-final.

'Mayo had won a Connacht Championship in 1981 but Kerry thrashed them and nobody got too excited about the future of the team. '85 was different. We should have beaten Dublin the first day but lacked experience. We had a young team and everybody knew that Mayo were back as a force. It was hugely important for the county and should have been the springboard to greater things but stupid things like cockiness got in the way. I look back at '86 and '87 as our lost years. That was when we should have consolidated our achievements but instead we went backwards. I still believe we were the best team in Connacht both years but Roscommon caught us on the hop in '86 and we lost a truly horrible Connacht final to Galway in '87.'

A broken leg caused McStay to miss the Connacht Championship triumph in 1988. 'In '89 I was struggling to get back to where I had been. I knew that when there were selection meetings there was discussion about my name. I was trying really hard and John O'Mahony gave me great support. In the Championship that year we got into the habit of winning tight matches in the last ten minutes. Johnno was always harping on about the last ten minutes and we felt we could really plough it. We felt we were invincible. In the All-Ireland semi-final we gave a very un-Mayo-like peformance when we wore Tyrone down. We thought we had a great chance going into the final.

'We were millimetres from winning the All-Ireland in '89. We hit the post twice and the ball bounced back into play. They hit the post twice but each time the ball went over the bar. One of their players double hopped the ball and scored a point but the ref, Paddy Collins who was normally an excellent referee, missed it. After scoring the goal, Anthony got another chance but the late John Kerins got a touch to it. The umpire backed away because he was afraid the ball was going to hit him. He missed John's touch and instead of giving us a forty-five, he flagged it wide. Our freetaker Michael Fitzmaurice was on fire that day and hadn't missed a placed ball, including a forty-five. If we had got a point at that stage it would have been a big help to us. Cork were a more experienced team than us, having contested the All-Ireland final the previous two years but they were very brittle at that stage of the game. As a forward, I could see their nerves in the way the backs were shouting at each other but we allowed them to settle rather than keep them on the ropes.'

In common with a whole generation of Mayo footballers McStay has special fondness for Anthony Finnerty.

'Three days after we lost the All-Ireland final to Cork everyone was very down. We were in Anthony's local pub, Mitchells, at about two o'clock in the afternoon and the place was packed. Someone asked him to say a few words to cheer them up. Anthony got up on a three-legged-stool and said, "I know ye all feel sorry for me and are cringing that I have to stand up like this in public but I've got to be positive and look on the bright side. If I had got that goal I missed, ye'd have been talking about me all winter but now that I missed it, ye'll never stop talking about me." Needless to say, he brought the house down.'

In selecting a dream team from Connacht, McStay's criteria were that they had to be people who he played with or against in the Connacht Championship during his playing days (1983–1990). He deliberately selected some of them out of position.

1. Eugene Lavin
(Mayo)

2. Martin Carney      3. Peter Ford      4. Jimmy Browne
(Mayo)                    (Mayo)              (Mayo)

5. Micheal Collins    6. Seamus McHugh    7. Dermot Flanagan
(Mayo)                    (Galway)             (Mayo)

8. Liam McHale                    9. T. J. Kilgallon
(Mayo)                                (Mayo)

10. Barry Brennan     11. Val Daly      12. Noel Durkan
(Galway)                  (Galway)           (Mayo)

13. Stephen Joyce    14. Paul Earley    15. Tony McManus
(Galway)                 (Roscommon)        (Roscommon)

# Big Mac

## Liam McHale

Brian McDonald was much maligned for his time in charge of the Mayo team but he was a formative influence in the career of Liam McHale.

'Basketball was my game when I was young. I had offers of scholarships to go to colleges in America. In 1985, I was brought on to the Mayo bench for the All-Ireland semi-final replay against Dublin. I had the catching and the other skills but I was lacking in the kicking department. Brian would take me for extra work in a one-to-one kicking session a few times a week during his lunchtime for a year and a half at the start of my senior career with Mayo. It was only when we got to the All-Ireland final in 1989 that I decided that I was really going to give football a serious go.

'That year holds very strong memories for me. My father died from cancer the day of the Connacht final. I rushed home after the game and he died ten minutes after I arrived. The next Sunday was the Connacht final replay against Roscommon. I scored four points and had one of my best games – though the All-Ireland semi-final against Tyrone was my best game for Mayo.

'Up to then, people in Mayo thought of me as "the basketballer". In 1989, I won some of them over but there were always a number of people who saw me as lacking the toughness that was needed for Gaelic football. I found it very strange but for some of them I "proved" myself in the Connacht final in 1993 when I was sent off for striking against Roscommon. I struck my opponent that day by accident and was horrified when I realised it but some of the Mayo fans thought I was making my mark at last and showing my steel. I found that attitude very sad.'

The Sam Maguire Cup remained as elusive as ever after 1989.

'I had given some thought to retiring because I was working my socks off and tired of us always falling short before John Maughan took over the Mayo job in 1995. I played with and against John and I really admired what he achieved in Clare. I thought he would make things happen and he was very unlucky not to have won an All-Ireland. At that stage, I had

developed into a leader of the team. I did a lot of directing of the team and was used to barking out orders from basketball. It suited John Maughan to have someone like that around.'

It was a case of so near and yet so far for McHale.

'1996 was my greatest year and my worst year. They say you make your own luck but we were unlucky.'

McHale was famously sent off in the All-Ireland final replay. 'I will never get over that. I felt I had no choice but to get involved. Fellas on my team were getting hit with haymakers and I was their leader and had a big bond with those guys. There was no way I could just stand back and watch and leave them to their own devices. If I had done nothing, I would not have been able to live with myself. If I was presented with those circumstances again, I would still do the same thing. I have a clear conscience because I didn't shirk my responsibility.'

McHale's regret about the sending off is tied in with his view of the way that game unfolded.

'Well, I believe the outcome would have been different if Meath had a midfielder sent off. When I went off, we had to get another midfielder on

*Left:* Mighty Mc: Liam McHale takes on Teddy McCarthy in the Cork defence in the 1989 All-Ireland final. *Photo:* Western People/*Henry Wills*

*Facing page:* Liam McHale is tackled by Offaly's Finbarr Cullen. *Photo:* Irish Examiner/*Des Barry*

which meant that we had to take Ray Dempsey off. Ray had scored 1-2 in the All-Ireland semi-final and was in great form so losing him was a blow. You have to remember we could only use three subs then. If Meath had lost a midfielder too, we wouldn't have had to replace Ray.'

Many people were surprised when McHale stated that getting sent off was akin to hearing that your mother had died.

'Losing an All-Ireland final is far worse than losing any other game. When you get that far and lose, especially to lose by a point in those circumstances, was sickening. We put in an astronomical effort, working very hard but had nothing to show for it.'

After McHale's retirement from football, John Maughan invited him to become a selector when Maughan had his second stint in charge of Mayo. 'In '89, '96 and '97 we were genuine contenders for an All-Ireland. When we got to the final in 2004 and 2006 we were over-achievers. We have seen since how good that Kerry team who beat us both those years is.'

The big midfielder tells a tale that he thinks is symptomatic of Mayo's fortunes in Croke Park in recent years.

'Before the 2004 All-Ireland final, I saw that there were great odds

# We need to talk about Kevin

## Kevin O'Neill

*Above:* Mayo's Kevin O'Neill has a shot at goal against Offaly at Croke Park.
*Photo:* Irish Examiner/*Des Barry*

I met Kevin O'Neill on a Saturday morning in early January at the River View Fitness Centre in Clonskeagh. Outside, Dublin is untypically quiet, as if the entire city is suffering from a collective Christmas hangover. Inside, Kevin has already clocked up an intensive training session.

Some players' careers are defined by a season. Kevin O'Neill is such a player. He won a Connacht title and an All-Star in his debut year in 1993 while he was still just a teenager. He seemed set to be the next big thing in Gaelic football but injuries intervened. So did John Maughan.

Football was in O'Neill's genes. In 1993, he made history when he became part of the first father and son partnership to win All-Star awards. His father, Liam, had won with Galway.

'It was only much later than I became aware of that. My father's inter-county playing career was over when I came on the scene but then he became manager of Mayo. I went everywhere with him including training sessions. It is not that I had major interaction with the Mayo players but I would stand behind the goals and kick the ball back to the likes of Willie Joe Padden, T. J. Kilgallon, Liam McHale and Padraig Brogan which was an unbelievable thrill for a kid. They were my heroes as well as Jack O'Shea and Larry Tompkins. The day of playing in my first Connacht final in '93, some of the senior players were checking to see if I was OK. To me it was as natural as riding a bike.'

A gap the size of a golf ball remains in his leg courtesy of a quad muscle injury sustained while he practised his frees the day before the Connacht final in 1994. To this day, he cannot take frees off the ground because of the injury. He received other serious injuries that ruined three seasons for him – a medial ligament injury in 1995 and a broken leg when he pushed hard for a place in the side the week before the 1997 All-Ireland final. 'Injuries like that make you stronger mentally and as you train long and hard to rehab, it makes you stronger physically. You also appreciate your football more when you come back after such bad injuries.'

In 1999, he was back in a familiar territory – languishing on the subs bench when Mayo lost to Cork in the All-Ireland semi-final, as he had in both the drawn game and replay in the 1996 All-Ireland final. The dictates of a demanding job with an international financial company took him to America for three years but he continued to commute home to play for his beloved Knockmore. When he returned to Ireland, he was unable to continue to travel regularly to Mayo because of work pressure so he transferred to play club football in Dublin with Na Fianna during John Maughan's second incarnation as Mayo manager.

'Playing club football in Dublin rejuvenated me and gave me a new

'We had great characters on the team like Anthony Finnerty. A sight to behold was Anthony doing his unique impersonation of Michael Flatley! Padraig Brogan was something else: both for his talent and his unique capacity to forget his teammates' names in big matches.

'We played Sligo one year in Gurteen in Sligo to officially open the local pitch. The parish priest came on the field to throw in the ball. It had been raining all morning and there was loads of surface water on the new pitch. Seán Maher our midfielder was not a man to stand back in any game whether it was a challenge game, training game or A versus B game. He was a real tough character on the field. Anyway, the local PP threw in the ball, Seán went up and caught it and proceeded to smash into the priest, landing the man of the cloth into a pool of water. That was Seán. He took no prisoners!'

O'Neill's dream team is:

1. Eugene Lavin
(Mayo)

2. Kenenth Mortimer
(Mayo)

3. Mick Lyons
(Meath)

4. Tony Scullion
(Derry)

5. Paul Curran
(Dublin)

6. Kieran McGeeney
(Armagh)

7. Seamus Moynihan
(Kerry)

8. Anthony Tohill
(Derry)

9. Darragh Ó Sé
(Kerry)

10. Kieran McDonald
(Mayo)

11. Larry Tompkins
(Cork)

12. Mickey Linden
(Down)

13. Maurice Fitzgerald
(Kerry)

14. Peter Canavan
(Tyrone)

15. Colm 'Gooch' Cooper
(Kerry)

Left: Keen Kevin: Kevin O'Neill acknowledges another characteristically sublime pass from Ciaran McDonald during the 2006 All-Ireland final against Kerry.

Keepers of the Flame

# The Lion with the Velvet Paw

## Bill Carlos

Listen to a small boy imitating his father's words, trying to get the sound right, the pitch and intonation, the vowels initially, and eventually, after many a difficult battle, those elusive consonants. Deep grammar or not – and the esteemed Mr Chomsky may well be correct about the structural mystery of language – what you are listening to is a young boy trying to forge a link with generations past, present and future. Perhaps if there is one reason why so many adults with big brains remain fascinated with sport in general and Gaelic games in particular. It is because we all start off as little creatures playing those games and, like salmon heading back from the sea, we never lose a sense of where the stream starts: in memories strung together which continue to mesmerise us. Gaelic games, unique in their evocative hold on identity, take us back to that moment of initial fascination with the world when as small, imitative children we first swung a hurley or kicked a ball. I believe that the mystery of human selfhood is bound up with the mystery of the GAA: 'how are we conscious?' and 'how do Gaelic games affect us?' are probably parts of the same bigger question for many of us, but we don't answer the first unless we answer the second. These are the thoughts that came hurtling into my head whenever I hear the name of Bill Carlos. That name is forever linked in my head with my father.

My most enduring memories of my father are of horses on summer days. He would carry a bag with two bottles of tea wrapped in two old stockings; a five-naggin whiskey bottle for himself and a naggin bottle for me as we went off to save the hay. When he took a break for his meal, he filled my head with stories of Roscommon's greatest footballers. The name that lodged deepest into my head was Bill Carlos because of his exotic

*Preceding page:* Follow the leader: Jack Mangan leads the Galway team before the 1956 All-Ireland final against Cork – J. Keeley, G. Daly, Tom Dillon, Jack Kissane, J. Mahon, M. Greally, Frank Eivers, Mattie McDonagh, J. Coyle, Seán Purcell, W. O'Neill, Joe Young and Frank Stockwell. Mattie McDonagh (ninth from the front) is the only Connacht footballer to have won four senior All-Ireland medals.

*Above:* Kicking king: (from left) Tom Gallagher (New York), Paddy Connell, Bill Carlos (with foot raised) and Meath's Brian Smith, Jimmy Reilly and Peter McDermott during the 1951 League final. *Photo:* Tony Conboy

nickname, 'the Lion with the Velvet Paw'. Although I never met Bill, I felt I knew him in a more intimate way than most of my relatives. When my father went to his grave when I was five, he left those conversations about Bill Carlos reverberating in my head.

Grace is but glory begun and glory is grace perfected. The late Bill Carlos made each game he played in Croke Park a day of grace and glory. He continues to occupy a hallowed place in the annals of the GAA, as the star centre-half-back on Roscommon's All-Ireland winning teams in 1943 and '44.

Yet Carlos gave me my biggest selection headache in this book: which Roscommon centre-half-back should I choose – Gerry O'Malley or Carlos? O'Malley was the star of the Roscommon team that caused a sensation in 1952 when they beat the great Mayo team that was led by Seán Flanagan which famously won All-Irelands in 1950 and '51. Because of a national newspaper strike, many people around the country only heard the result on the Tuesday after the game, and when they did most thought it was a mistake.

*Above:* Two of the greats: Roscommon legend Dermot Earley with Bill Carlos (right) at a special meeting of the Roscommon supporters in Dublin.

Given his stature in the game all neutrals wanted the 1962 All-Ireland final to be 'Gerry O'Malley's All-Ireland', only for Roscommon's star player to be injured in the game and Kerry to beat the men in primrose and blue by 1-6 to 1-12. The passage of time has allowed O'Malley to see the black humour in the occasion.

'I had to be taken to hospital after the All-Ireland and I was in a bed beside a man I had never met before. My "neighbour" knew who I was and we got to talking, the way you do. The next day a fella came in with the newspapers who didn't recognise me from Adam and my new friend asked him, "How did the papers say O'Malley played?"

"Brutal," came the instant reply and it certainly left me feeling even more brutal!'

One of O'Malley's most attractive qualities is his ability to tell stories against himself. Gerry was also a wonderful hurler. At one stage, he played for Connacht against Munster in a Railway Cup match. At the time the balance of power in hurling was heavily weighted towards Munster but Connacht ran them close enough. On the way home he stopped off for a drink with the legendary Galway hurler, Inky Flaherty. Given the interest in hurling in the Banner County the barman recognised Inky straight away and said,

'Ye did very well.'

'Not too bad,' replied Inky.

'I supose if it wasn't for O'Malley you would have won,' speculated the barman.

Flaherty answered back, 'Here he is beside me. Ask him yourself.'

In the end, a conversation with the late Jimmy Murray resolved the thorny selection issue for me. Just to be in his company made me feel that the world was in season and I have complete faith in his judgement. He answered with typical diplomacy:

'How am I to choose the greatest Roscommon centre-half-back between Bill Carlos and Gerry O'Malley? When Bill retired it was a huge blow for Roscommon and I suppose many of us felt we would never see his like again but lucky enough, within a short time we discovered another great star in Gerry O'Malley. I don't really think you can or should compare players from different eras and it's not fair to either Gerry or Bill to compare one against the other. Both were superb players over a long number of years and both had tremendous dedication. But as you put the gun to my head, I have to opt for Bill.

'I would go as far as saying Bill was one of the greatest centre-backs I ever saw playing in any era and that he stands ahead of maybe all the great Roscommon footballers. You have to remember that when he won a National League medal with New York in 1950 he became, and remains, the only Roscommon player to win both All-Ireland medals and National League medals. From his earliest days wearing the primrose-and-blue jersey it was obvious he was something special. As a teenager he won All-Ireland colleges medals in hurling and football with Connacht when he was a student in Roscommon CBS. He was only twenty-one when he won his first senior All-Ireland medal in 1943 but you would never have known it because of his extraordinary maturity physically and every other way.

'Given his height, strength, fetch, mobility, anticipation, positional sense and his long accurate kick from hand or ground, he was the complete centre-back. It was often said, that when playing with Bill we felt like bringing a chair to relax in, whenever the ball was going near Bill!

'It was immaterial how the ball came to him – high or low, left or right, carried or kicked – Bill invariably collected it. Sometimes he came bursting through with it, sometimes he came through side-stepping to avoid the forward rushes but he came away to clear it. And when Bill cleared the ball, it stayed cleared for quite a while!

'It was also his firm contention that forwards can be prevented from scoring without infringing any of the rules. He was a strong believer in sportsmanship. Bill felt that at the very longest, it was only a very short period really that you'd be playing the game, so it should always be played properly for everyone's enjoyment.

'Bill loved being in the action. When the ball was up at the other goal I think he was longing for it to be at his end even if it meant danger. There is one thing you need in any position and that's anticipation. His intention was always to close down all traffic to the goal. You cannot afford to allow anything to develop in the play, otherwise anything can happen and you are in trouble. Bill was always blessed with good anticipation, but he never relaxed. He was always on his toes even when the ball was way up the field.

'His biggest asset, and he had lots of them, was his ability to read the game. I never knew how he knew where the ball was going but he did. He'd be out to the ball like a bullet. If you waited, the other fella had as good a chance as you of getting it. That's why Bill never looked for his man at any time, the ball was always all he was interested in. When the ball came in, his man was looking for him but Bill was already clearing the ball.'

Bill was a native of Ballintubber and played club football with Tarmon. He won an All-Ireland minor medal and captained the minor team to All-Ireland glory in 1941.

Few people observed Carlos at such close quarters as his half-back teammate Brendan Lynch. 'If I was going into battle the one player I would choose would be Bill Carlos. He had the heart of a lion but was a gentleman to his fingertips. When the chips were down Bill would always come through for you. I was lucky to play beside him for so long. I could not have had a better minder.'

Bill Carlos died in Florida in 1997. To many, his definitive epitaph was that of the late Cardinal Tomás O'Fiaich who, when he was asked what he would like to have achieved as a sportsman, stated: 'To play centre-back like Bill Carlos.'

Fittingly, Carlos was on the Roscommon Team of the Millennium. For the record that team in full was:

1. Aidan Brady

| 2. Harry Keegan | 3. Pat Lindsay | 4. Bill Jackson |
| 5. Brendan Lynch | 6. Bill Carlos | 7. Phelim Murray |

8. Gerry O'Malley          9. Eamon Boland

| 10. Dermot Earley | 11. Jimmy Murray | 12. Donal Keenan |
| 13. Tony McManus | 14. Jack McQuillan | 15. John Joe Nerney |

# History Maker

## Jack Mangan

The most striking thing about talking with Jack Mangan is that he laughs heartily and laughs often. At eighty years of age he is a double amputee, having lost both legs below the knees through diabetes, or more precisely peripheral vascular disease. Adversity is no stranger to Mangan. When he was twelve years old he broke his ankle very badly and was told by doctors that he should quit football. He responded by having a special boot made and played on with the ankle heavily bandaged. In 1957, he contracted pneumonia while away with the Galway team in New York. Despite being weak and not have trained, he ignored medical advice imploring him not to play against Louth when they returned to Ireland but he gave such a stellar display that he was made 'Sports Star of the Week'.

For the last thirty years, he has been based in England though he continues to 'come home' to Ireland at Christmas and a few times during the year to visit family and former teammates like Gerry Kirwan and Tom Dillon. He made history by becoming the first goalkeeper to lift the Sam Maguire Cup when he captained Galway in 1956.

'That time you couldn't pick a ball off the ground. If you dived on the ball, you had to get up and put your toe under it and lift it. There was some chance of that in a goalmouth. People think it is a big responsibility but being a goalie never bothered me. My attitude was if you saved it, you saved it and if some fella scored against you, he scored. If I ever let in a soft goal, though, I would be very upset for letting down the team. There was way more body contact then which I relished, as it made the game very exciting. Mind you, if you lost possession, you couldn't drop on the ball, so sometimes you had no option but to concede a penalty.'

Mangan made his inter-county debut against Waterford when he was nineteen years old but his big reputation in the world of Gaelic football rests significantly on his performance in the 1956 All-Ireland semi-final. On foot of a convincing campaign in Connacht, Galway were hot favourites to win but Tyrone were not taking any prisoners on their Croke Park debut.

Mangan came in for some close attention and three times he was pinned against the goalpost in possession. He managed to clear without loss of a goal or conceding a fifty. Ultimately, the game boiled down to a showdown between Tyrone's greatest footballer, with the possible exception of Peter Canavan, Iggy Jones and Mangan. Before his death, Jones reflected on the game. It was a match that he was never allowed to forget.

'I had a goal chance to win the game when we were trailing by just two points. I made a run and cut along the in-line. You don't score goals from there so I was looking for a teammate to pass to but there was no Tyrone forward there for me. I remember cutting in from the in-line and getting on to the edge of the small parallelogram. The Galway goalie Jack Mangan was toward the near post. I thought to myself, "I'll not get it past him but I'll get it over him." I punched the ball in the opposite direction to which I was travelling and over his head. Unfortunately, Mangan was very agile and somehow got his hand to it. Thirty years later, I went to a school to speak to the children and this boy came up to me and said, "My dad told me you were the man that lost the All-Ireland for Tyrone".'

Mangan plays down the crucial significance of his agility.

'Galway won by 0-8 to 0-6 and that was all that matters. After that, we had a feeling it was going to be our year. The atmosphere was electric the day of the final. I just can't describe the feeling. It was like being in a different world. From the throw-in, it was immediately apparent that it was going to be a cracking game. Seán Purcell and Frank Stockwell were on fire. Frank was finishing everything Seán was giving him.'

Mangan's acceptance speech is considered one of the greatest ever heard in Croke Park, together with those of Anthony Daly and Joe Connolly. 'While Cork had a reputation for being hard they played a very clean game and I said that if any youngster wanted to know how football should be played, they should follow the example of the Cork team.'

Seán Purcell found it difficult to decide whether he admired Mangan most as a goalkeeper or as a man. 'He was as good as we've ever seen. He had this mighty leap off the ground and was the archetypal safe pair of hands. To be honest, if he was playing now, I don't think anybody would ever score against him because of the way goalies are protected, you might even say mollycoddled, today. In those days, you'd forwards and backs all coming in on top of him and Jack would come out on top of everything and soar through the air through the mêlée and grab the ball or at least punch it to safety. He had great guts. He was scared of nothing and would go in where no sane person would to protect the goal. The best thing, though, was that he had the sharpest eye I've ever seen which left him with such great anticipation

*Left:* My ball: Jack Mangan thwarts the Cork defence and emerges with the ball in the 1956 All-Ireland final. Tommy Furling in the Number 13 jersey falls to the ground. *Centre:* Safety first: Jack Mangan claims the ball despite fierce Cork pressure in the 1956 All-Ireland final. Niall Fitzgerald and Denis 'Tooth' Kelleher are on the right. Jack Kissane (fifth from left) runs into help.
*Right:* The dropping ball: Galway goalie Jack Mangan is poised to claim the ball in the 1956 All-Ireland final in front of 70,772 spectators. Cork forward Johnny Creedon looks up in despair while Tom Dillon (in the number 4 jersey) waits for the ball.

that he could make a really difficult save look very easy. I will never forget his speech that day in Croke Park. It showed what a sportsman he was. He commanded such respect and he had great judgement. Only a broken collarbone stopped him from playing in the 1957 National League final. It was he who recommended the switch between Frank Stockwell and myself, which led to our winning goal that day. He had great dedication. He was offered the chance to play soccer for Drumcondra but he turned it down.'

When asked about the greatest player he ever saw, Mangan's answer comes with lightning speed.

'Seán Purcell was the best. We were from the same street in Tuam. I took the captaincy off him after a vote. Although I felt bad for him, he didn't hold it against me and we remained the best of friends. He was a natural with a wonderful temperament. If we were behind we would always rely on him to do domething special. The next best I would have seen was another Tuam man, Frank Stockwell. The two of them didn't even have to look for each other on the field of play, they knew each other so well. Outside Galway the two greatest players I would have seen would be Mayo's Padraic Carney and Tom Langan. I always enjoyed meeting the Kerry lads. The social aspect of the game is one of my fondest memories. It was more leisurely then and had a lot more humour than now. I haven't seen that much football since I left Ireland. I am not that keen on all the passing that goes on today.

'I know I was lucky to win an All-Ireland medal. There have been so many great players who didn't. I think you will find that there are more Connacht footballers on the Centenary team of greatest players never to have won an All-Ireland than anywhere else.'

That team was:

1. Aidan Brady
(Roscommon)

| 2. Willie Casey | 3. Eddie Boyle | 4. John McKnight |
|:---:|:---:|:---:|
| (Mayo) | (Louth) | (Armagh) |
| 5. Gerry O'Reilly | 6. Gerry O'Malley | 7. Seán Quinn |
| (Wicklow) | (Roscommon) | (Armagh) |

8. Jim McKeever      9. Tommy Murphy
(Derry)      (Laois)

| 10. Seán O'Connell | 11. Packy McGarty | 12. Micheál Kearins |
|:---:|:---:|:---:|
| (Derry) | (Leitrim) | (Sligo) |
| 13. Charlie Gallagher | 14. Willie McGee | 15. Dinny Allen |
| (Cavan) | (Mayo) | (Cork) |

# Gone Too Soon

## John Morley

O f all the matches I have attended the one that stands out most in my memory is the Connacht final of 1980. The game is more memorable for the emotion it generated than because of the actual contest on the pitch. Uniquely, the two opposing teams were united in grief for a favourite son on both sides of the county border.

In 1975 Sligo had one of their finest hours when they defeated Mayo in the Connacht final replay. Seán Kilbride, a Mayo star of the time who subsequently played with great distinction for Roscommon, attributes Mayo's defeat to one factor – the absence of John Morley and specifically, the failure of the powers that be to lure him out of retirement. Kilbride feels that John's experience was the missing link in what was potentially a very good Mayo team.

It has become a cliché for journalists and broadcasters to refer to a particular player's 'cultured left foot'. Yet every cliché has its truth and from the days when he first sprang to prominence with St Jarlath's College, Tuam, where he won All-Ireland College's senior medals in both 1960 and '61 there was never any doubt that John Morley's left foot merited this sobriquet. This reputation was enhanced when he made his first appearance in the Mayo colours in Charlestown in 1961. His former teammate Willie McGee recalls, 'John was always getting slagged about his right leg but he always defended it by saying that without it he couldn't use his left.'

Morley's versatility was such that he could play in almost any position for Mayo, though he played mostly at centre-back. He played a then record 112 senior games for the county up to 1974, captaining Mayo to their first Connacht senior title in 12 years, and also starring in 1969 winning side. In the same years he helped Connacht to Railway Cup successes.

The most famous incident in his illustrious career came in the 1970 League final clash when Mayo defeated Down. John was playing at centre-half-back, when a Down player grabbed him and tore his shorts. Just as he was about to put his foot into fresh shorts, the ball came close by, he

*Top:* You raise me up: John Morley celebrates Mayo's Connacht triumph in 1969 in McHale Park, Castlebar, County Mayo, and, *(below)* In the line of duty: John Morley in a professional capacity in 1978.

abandoned his shorts and, in his briefs, fielded the ball and cleared it heroically down the field to the adulation of the crowd.

Former Roscommon great Dermot Earley frequently came up against John but his outstanding memory of him comes from a match they played together.

'We played together for Connacht and having won the Railway Cup in 1969, we went out to New York to play in the Cardinal Cushing Games. In our first game against New York in Boston, I was playing very well in midfield. On one occasion, the ball was hanging in the air. I went into the clouds, or so I thought, to catch the ball. I touched the ball and then it was wrenched from my hands. As I reached the ground, I turned around quickly to be on the defensive, but I looked around to see that it as my teammate John Morley with the ball tucked in as tight as could be, ready to set up another attack. You would have to consider him as being one of the great players.

'In the west of Ireland there are two things we are known for. One is for saying "mighty". The other thing we are noted for, is that we generally refer to people we admire, even though we may never have met them, by their surname. If you go into any GAA setting in the West of Ireland today, indeed all the West of Ireland is a GAA setting and you say "Morley", everyone will know the name. He remains known by that name with affection and admiration.'

Inevitably, any discussion on John Morley's career is overshadowed by the tragic circumstances of his death. The man who gave every ounce of energy on the playing field for Mayo, was prepared to put his life on the line to honour his professional duty and uphold law and order regardless of any risk to his personal safety. The bravery which he had so often exhibited in the green and red of Mayo was to manifest itself even more strikingly in the dark blue uniform of the Garda Síochána. A hero in life became a hero in death.

John was murdered on 7 July 1980 along with a fellow native of Knock, Henry Byrne. He was just thirty-seven years of age. Another Mayo man and centre-forward for Michael Glaveys, Derek Kelly was injured in the incident. John had initially been based in Ballaghaderreen on the Mayo-Roscommon border before moving to Roscommon town and finally to Castlerea. In all three places, he had fully immersed himself in all manner of community activities.

A robbery had taken place, in a time when the IRA were involved in a campaign to rob banks, and the squad car encountered the getaway car at the crossroads outside Loughlynn on the way to Ballaghaderreen. Shots were fired and Henry Byrne and John Morley were fatally wounded. First on the scene was a retired garda, the late Garda Kneafsey. Interviewed on the RTÉ news that night, he said he had arrived on the scene to discover a guard wounded and badly bleeding on the side of the road and that he had recognised him immediately as 'the footballer'. He spoke to him but the man was shaking as if registering arrows of pain shooting through his now frail body. John had said to him, 'I'm getting awful cold' which indicated a loss of blood. Then Garda Kneafsey said an Act of Contrition. Shortly after, the ambulance arrived but it was too late to save John.

The tragedy had a huge effect on Connacht because the Connacht final was the following Sunday. It was between Mayo and Roscommon, between a county that John had played for, and the county he had lived in for many years. Everybody in both counties respected him. That Connacht final played in brilliant weather in an exceptionally bad summer on 13 July reflected that feeling. Fr Leo Morahan, who was on the Connacht Council at the time, gave a poignant and moving oration before the throw-in. In the circumstances, Roscommon's 3-13 to 0-8 win hardly seemed to matter.

In 1997, John was chosen at centre-back on the *Western People's* Best Mayo Team 1960–1990. The team in full was as follows:

1. Eugene Rooney

2. Willie Casey     3. Ray Prendergast     4. Dermot Flanagan

5. Johnny Carey     6. John Morley     7. Eamon Walsh

8. Willie Joe Padden     9. T. J. Kilgallon

10. Joe Langan     11. John Gibbons     12. Joe Corcoran

13. Martin Carney     14. Willie McGee     15. J. J. Cribbins

# Rock Solid

## Harry Keegan

During his seventeen-year inter-county career, Harry Keegan played scores of games for Roscommon, from an All-Ireland final to challenge games. The shared characteristic of those games is that all Harry's performances had the intensity of a medieval martyr. Despite his toughness he got only one booking in his playing days.

Yet his career almost perished before it begun.

'I made an inauspicious debut for Roscommon in a League match in 1972 against Kilkenny. A few months later, we played Galway in the Connacht semi-final in Roscommon. We were leading by twelve points at half-time and the perception was that the referee gave everything to Galway. John Tobin kicked frees for fun and the match ended in a draw. The crowd were incensed and broke through the fences to attack the referee. It was a real mob scene. John Morley was on duty that day and stood in front of the referee and, only for that, he might have been killed or certainly very badly injured. The ref was struck, though, and Martin Silke and myself were accused of hitting him. Martin was a sub for us that day. In fact, the ref was hit but by another Roscommon sub. We were brought up before the Connacht Council. It was very serious for Martin as he was a garda and if he had been found guilty of assault, it would have major repercussions for his career. Likewise, I had just begun my nursing career in St Ita's Portrane and if a finding of assault was upheld against me, it would have been very damaging professionally.

'The maddening thing was when the incident happened I was thirty yards away. I had been marking Seamus Leydon that day and he wrote a letter to the Connacht Council. The night of the inquiry, Seán Purcell spoke on my behalf as well. The frustrating thing was neither the referee nor the umpires turned up. We were put through all that stress for nothing.

'We beat Galway in the replay in Tuam. Tom Heneghan was put on John Tobin that day and Tobin didn't get a smell of the ball. Heneghan was the perfect man to put manners on a player like Tobin.'

*Above:* No place for the faint-hearted: Harry Keegan (on the right) tackles Dublin's Kieran Duff. Pat Lindsay is on his knees in this National League match in 1983.

The All-Ireland semi-final that year proved significant for Keegan. 'I got my right ankle injured that day and the injury was to persecute me for the rest of my career. I had to go off and we were badly beaten. We trained very hard for that game but left our fitness on the training ground. We were really flying two weeks after. The game is probably most remembered for the long time Mick O'Connell sat down in the middle of the pitch tying his laces. To some people in Roscommon, it was a bit disrespectful.'

Keegan is the only Roscommon player to have won three All-Star awards. However, it is another trip to America that stands out for him rather than his trips with the All-Stars.

'Long before Cork made striking fashionable in the GAA, we were the first to threaten to use player power. We were in New York to play Kerry in the Cardinal Cushing Games over two matches. We beat them initially in a thirteen-a-side in the first game. We had been promised money from John Kerry O'Donnell who was "Mr GAA" in New York. We knew for a fact that Kerry had been paid but we got nothing and we were running short of money. A council of war was held by the Roscommon players, appropriately under Dermot Earley. The word was sent back to John Kerry – no money, no playing. As far as I know, we were the first county to threaten to strike!

'Another memory I have of the trip is that we were invited to a formal reception hosted by the Lord Mayor. It was a real big deal for the County Board. The problem was that the heat was almost unbearable. One of the lads brought down a keg of beer to keep himself distracted from the heat! The late Gerry Beirne went so far as to take off his shirt, which was a major breach of protocol. The message quickly came down from the top table from the county chairman, Michael O'Callaghan, to get it back on quickly.'

The American influence was soon felt in an unexpected way in Roscommon when team coach Seán Young asked the players to kneel down and say a prayer before running out on the pitch. Harry Keegan was nonplussed. 'That kind of thing is big in American football.'

Keegan is very appreciative of the role played by the Roscommon County Board, although he feels that their methods were unorthodox.

'They always looked after us even if the money wasn't too generous. One incident stands out for me. After a Connacht final in the '70s I went to one of the top officials in the County Board and told him that I needed money for expenses. He brought me out to his car, opened the boot and pulled out a one-hundred-pound note from a green wellington and handed it to me. He then told me to send in the docket for it.'

In 1977, Roscommon played Armagh in the All-Ireland semi-final. It is not the loss in the replay that most irks Keegan today.

'Everybody keeps talking about the Kerry-Dublin semi-final that

year and it's regularly shown on TV but people forget that we produced two great entertaining games, which almost a hundred-thousand people came to watch. Yet neither of the games is ever shown on television. The other so-called "classic" was really a game of rugby league, there was so much hand-passing. We played Armagh again in the 1980 semi-final and that was a very entertaining, high-scoring game but it is never shown on TV whereas our final in 1980 is shown, even though it is a much poorer game.'

Clashes between Armagh and Roscommon would continue to provide many memorable moments down the years. In 1982, they met for a series of three matches in America. Before the first match, some of the players had partied too hard and went onto the pitch in something less than the full of their health. At one point, the ball was coming in towards the Armagh goal. Their accomplished full-back Jim Kerr went for the ball but was experiencing a form of double vision and he went up for the ball but caught an imaginary one instead, toe-tapped it and cleared it. Meanwhile, a Roscommon player caught the real ball and stuck it in the net. When interrogated about the mishap, Kerr's response contained no admission of guilt, 'I got the ball I went for!'

Keegan has one particularly strong memory of playing Armagh.

'We played them in a fierce match in the League at the height of the Troubles. There was a skirmish and a lot of "scelping" in that match. They beat us by a point. We were delighted they beat us because there were rocks and stones raining down on us after the game in the dressing room. What would they have done if we won! It was not one of my favourite places to go as they were one of the few crowds I found abusive. I'm sure the Troubles did have an impact on them but I couldn't understand why they took it out on Roscommon above any team.'

Despite his long service to the county, Keegan missed out on the

*Left:* Get your hands off: Harry Keegan (third from left) claims the ball in a National League match against Cork as Roscommon's Gerry Mannion (far left) and Cork legend Jimmy Barry Murphy (second from left) look on. *Photo:* Tony Conboy
*Facing page:* Prince Harry: Harry Keegan (second from left) looks aghast as Kerry's Jack O'Shea shoots goalwards in the 1978 All-Ireland semi-final. Tom Heneghan (near right) makes a vain attempt to block the ball.

county's national title in that era.

'I was a mere bystander in the National League in 1979 because of a hamstring injury. Hamstrings were the bane of my life. During training, I would have to hold myself back to try and protect them but I gave it all in the games. I really had to mind myself and there was no drinking, especially because I was living and working in Dublin and I had a lot of travel to deal with.

'I was surprised we beat Cork so easily in that League final. Cork had a team of stars, including Jimmy Barry-Murphy who was lethal from twelve yards but Tom Heneghan had him in his pocket that day. I didn't tog out which was a mistake because I didn't feel like part of the squad. The only time the team went up the steps of the Hogan stand to collect a Cup I was in the crowd.

'We lost the All-Ireland semi-final to Dublin later that year. It was our third year in a row to lose a semi-final and that does play on your mind. You wonder if you will ever make it. We only lost by a point but it was a case of so near yet so far. We didn't have the killer instinct to put them away when the game was ours for the taking. I always felt that in those sort of games the referee gave the benefit of the doubt to the "big counties" like Dublin.'

A more crushing disappointment came in 1980 when Roscommon lost the All-Ireland to Kerry by three points, having raced in to a good lead early on.

'What stays with me is that there was no real celebration from the Kerry players nor the fans. That's what hurt me the most. Winning had become so routine it didn't seem to matter to them. When they won in 1997, you could see it did matter to the Kerry lads because they hadn't won an All-Ireland for eleven years at that stage.'

Keegan pulls no punches when giving the reasons for Roscommon's fall from grace the next year when they lost to Sligo in the Connacht Championship.

'Sligo was a disaster. I was very annoyed with certain players, with a few of the forwards who were not right, nor focused. I knew from events beforehand that some of our players we depended the most on were not up for the game the way Sligo were. At that stage, we needed to get some new blood coming into the team but we had no new talent coming through.'

In 1986, Keegan almost single-handedly won a Connacht title for Roscommon with a vintage display. An injury late in the game saw him leaving the pitch and his immediate opponent took advantage of the situation to score a late winning goal for Galway.

'I always hated marking Stephen Joyce because he was so small!

That day, though, he wasn't giving me any problems. The really annoying thing about that game was that I had warned the county board that someone would get injured because there was a hole in the pitch but nobody did anything about it. In the end, it was me who ran into it and I busted my right ankle. The pain was horrific and I had to go off and Stephen won the game for Galway but it could have been avoided.'

Despite his retirement from inter-county football in 1988 Keegan continues to play an active role in club football in Dublin with Fingallians. There, he formed a friendship with one of the game's more controversial characters.

'I played for years with Kieran Duff who was one of the most talented half-forwards I have ever seen. I believe he was more sinned against than sinning. I think the incident in the 1983 All-Ireland final when he appeared to try and kick a Galway player in the head looked an awful lot worse than it was. It wasn't like Brian Mullins who nearly broke Brian Talty's jaw. Duff gave everything for the county and for us in club games. That didn't endear him to people. In club matches, lots of Dubs fans would be baying for his blood!'

A League match against Dublin provided Keegan with the most amusing moment of his career.

'The week before, I played against Charlie Redmond in a club match and he was sensational. Charlie, though, did not like close attention. He was a big man but was a bit soft and didn't like the physical stuff. If you gave him a yard, he would destroy you. I managed to get a clatter in on him and he went down like a sack of spuds. One of his own players came running up to him and said: "Get up you f**ker, he didn't hit you half hard enough."'

Keegan's dream team is:

1. Charlie Nelligan
(Kerry)

2. Jimmy Deenihan      3. Mick Lyons       4. Robbie Kelleher
(Kerry)                (Meath)              (Dublin)

5. Kevin McCabe        6. Kevin Moran       7. Liam Currams
(Tyrone)               ( Dublin)            (Offaly)

8. Jack O'Shea                    9. Brian Mullins
(Kerry)                           (Dublin)

10. Matt Connor      11. Denis 'Ogie' Moran       12. Pat Spillane
(Offaly)             (Kerry)                       (Kerry)

13. Jimmy Barry Murphy   14. Jimmy Keaveney       15. John Egan
(Cork)                   (Dublin)                  (Kerry)

# Mayo's Man Mountain

## T. J. Kilgallon

T. J. Kilgallon's first taste of success came in 1978 when he was on the Mayo team that beat a star-laden Dublin side that included Barney Rock and Kieran Duff to win the All-Ireland minor final. Two years later, he found himself lining out at midfield in the Connacht senior final.

'I was only eighteen and it was a real baptism of fire. I was marking Dermot Earley. He wasn't that big but he had massive shoulders and legs and, to be honest, I was a bit intimidated in his company. They trounced us but Dermot made a point of seeking me out after the game to shake my hand. He was a real gentleman. I think the only player I have seen with stronger legs was Harry Keegan. We played Roscommon in 1983 and Harry shouldered me, completely fairly, but left me completely winded.'

In 1985 Kilgallon and Mayo got their revenge.

'When I broke into the Mayo team first we had no real management but in 1982, Liam O'Neill took charge of us and brought us up to the mark. Roscommon had given us many a hiding, so in '85 we were determined we would "dog into them" and match them physically. We beat them convincingly.

'Although we lost in a replay to Dublin in the All-Ireland semi-final, it was a real learning experience and a first for a lot of the players. One of the things I remember is one of our selectors Billy Fitzpatrick, who was forty-one, coming on and scoring a point. Despite his age, he had only played ten or twelve games for Mayo.'

The following year, Mayo fans and players had great expectations for the Connacht Championship after the apparent breakthrough in 1985.

'Ten days before we faced Roscommon we played Cavan in a challenge and we were brilliant. However, before the Roscommon game Dermot Flanagan got shingles and we ended up playing the game without five other key players because of injuries. We were missing the spine of our team and were flat on the day and the Rossies beat us. I was talking to Martin Carney about this recently and we agreed that if there had been a

*Above:* Roving forward: T. J. Kilgallon breaks through the Sligo defence in characteristic style. *Photo:* Western People/*Henry Wills*.

backdoor that year we would have done really, really well because we had been flying before the Roscommon game and if we got our injured players back, we would have mounted a strong challenge for Sam.

'That's probably the big regret of my career. In '86 and '87 a lot of us were at our peak but on neither occasion did we deliver on our potential. We were a very skilful team and in our prime, more so than when we got to the final in '89 and I see those two years as the time we really missed the boat. Emigration was a problem. We lost some good players like Eugene Griffin and an outstanding player in Ger Geraghty. Both Liam O'Neill and John O'Mahony tried to get him back and it nearly happened a few times but he never made it.'

Things improved in 1988.

'When John O'Mahony came in to manage us, he was a confident man who believed in his own ability. He brought new ways and new ideas. Meath beat us in the All-Ireland semi-final but we ran them close and that gave us hope that better things were coming.'

1989 saw Kilgallon in an unfamiliar role.

'The year started badly for me. I severed my medial ligament and there was a possibility that I would never play again. Our physio, Martin Carney's wife, did a great job with me but when I got back to fitness Willie Joe Padden and Seán Maher were going very well at midfield. In my life I only ever played three games at centre-half-back but they were a Connacht final replay; an All-Ireland semi-final and an All-Ireland final. The first time was against Roscommon and I went back to my spot to pick up Eamon McManus Jnr. He turned and said to me: "I think you're in the wrong place." I had a bit of a laugh with him about it. It wasn't that he was playing mind games or anything.'

So who did play mind games?

'Meath. Gerry McEntee would always stand nearer the opposing free-taker than he was supposed to and would try and put the kicker off by saying something like: "You're going to miss." He would tell you that you would put it to the right or the left but never over the bar. Colm O'Rourke was not shy on the field. He would always be passing a smart comment to you. Some of the lads thought he was trying to get you irked enough to punch him so that you would be sent off. He was certainly trying to distract you and put you off your game. I think Ryan McMenamin is probably the main exponent of that "art" today.'

The 1989 All-Ireland is yet another case of what might have been for Mayo. 'After Anthony Finnerty got the goal, we were in the driving seat because having lost the previous two years they were starting to doubt themselves but in the last ten minutes, we went into disarray and let them off the hook. They finished strongly and got the final three points.

'There were ten-thousand people waiting for us when we flew back to Knock. It was awfully moving. There was a real party atmosphere and we went on the beer for three or four days to kill the pain. There was none of the back-stabbing you normally have after a defeat. It was almost a mini-celebration and Mayo people were proud of us for getting there and playing well. There was a feeling that we needed to do a tour of the county as a political move as much as anything else. I went back to work on the Wednesday, though, because for me it was over and done with – but not achieved.'

Mayo's next attempt at redemption came in the All-Ireland semi-final in 1992. 'There was kind of a bad vibe all year and even though we won the Connacht final there was a sense in the camp that things were not going well. Probably the most memorable incident that happened in that game was that Enon Gavin broke the crossbar in Castlebar and the match had to be delayed. The management had brought back Padraig Brogan earlier that year – I'm not saying it was a popular move with the players. When we played Donegal in the All-Ireland semi-final it was probably the worst game ever seen in Croke Park. Padraig had played for Donegal the previous year and when the Donegal lads saw him warming up, you could see that it gave them new energy.

'Things got ugly after that. It was more personal than it should have been. It was probably an early example of player power. We said that if there wasn't a change of management a lot of us would walk away. I was asked recently if we really did spend a training session pushing cars. We did! It was in the Dunnes Stores car-park in Castlebar and the cars were really big. There was not a great humour in the camp and the manager had to walk the plank. John O'Mahony had stepped down in 1991 because he was not let choose his own selectors and maybe that's when we should have acted.'

Kilgallon won an All-Star in 1992 and the following year, he played his last match in a county jersey.

'Jack O'Shea's appointment as manager generated a lot of enthusiasm in the county. We won the Connacht final. I was brought on as a sub that day and felt I had made a good contribution. I was fuming when I wasn't chosen in the starting team against Cork in the All-Ireland semi-final and felt like not turning up on the day. On the Thursday before the game my quad muscle went astray. I was asked at half-time if I was OK to go on and I replied that I would give it a go but, understandably, they decided not to risk me. The last ten minutes of that match was probably the low point of Mayo football as we stopped playing and Cork stuffed us by 5-15 to 0-10. Although I was only thirty-two I had a lot of mileage on the clock and retired.'

He left with many happy memories to treasure of his colleagues in the green and red. 'One incident probably sums up the tight bond we had. We went for a holiday trip to the Canaries and one night Jimmy Burke was in a night club when a guy stole his wallet and ran outside with Jimmy chasing after him. Three of us happened to be coming in the opposite direction and we chased the thief into an alley. I'm six foot two but I was the smallest of our foursome. The guy had no escape and turned very contrite and handed the wallet back saying: "Your wallet, sir." Let's just say it wasn't left at that!'

T. J. is proof of the old adage that the going to a wedding is the making of another. In his case the love of his life is an RTÉ personality.

'I met Eileen Magnier in 1990 and we got married two years later.

She had no background in football. She's from Kilkenny and she's a cousin of Joe Hennessey. Whenever we are out, young people know Eileen because she's often on the news but they generally have no idea who I am. The odd time you hear someone say: "He used to play football" and the galling thing is when the person they are talking to doesn't believe them because I don't look the part any more!'

Even before he stopped playing, Kilgallon had made his mark as a coach in Sligo. He was teaching in Summerhill College at the time and, together with fellow teacher Peter Ford, he took the school to an All-Ireland A Colleges final in 1985.

'It was a great buzz. Our star player was Donie McDonagh who was the best minor I had ever seen. He went on a soccer scholarship to America. Two years after that some of the lads I had taught and coached were on the Sligo senior panel and I was playing against them.'

After his retirement, Kilgallon enjoyed success in club management in both Mayo and Sligo but that was put on hold when an old friend came calling.

'In 2000, Peter Ford rang me after he was appointed manager in Sligo and asked me to be one of his selectors. Although we were very close friends I said no. I later said no a second time but finally after a third call I said yes. You must remember that Galway had beaten Sligo by 0-22 to 0-4 in the Connacht semi-final in Markievicz Park that year. When we took over in Sligo morale was very low. We invited a panel of twenty-four to our first training session but only fourteen trained. Ten players had very lame excuses. Peter and I looked each other in the eye that evening and wondered what kind of a mess we had walked ourselves into but things got going then and we had two great years, though, I believe we left the Connacht final in 2002 behind us. We picked the wrong team and took tremendous flak for it but beating Tyrone shortly after revived things dramatically. By 2003, though, things had gone flat and a new voice was needed, so when our three years were up we gave no thought to the possibility of staying on.'

During his career T. J. witnessed some bizarre events.

'We were playing Galway in the Connacht Championship when Tomás Tierney "did a job" on Kevin McStay. Kevin was badly injured and had to go off. I was friends with Tomás and had shared a house with him at one stage but I couldn't believe that the referee, Seán Mullaney from Roscommon, wasn't booking him. I confronted Seán about it and he told me that the reason was that he had lost his notebook and couldn't book Tomás without it!'

Kilgallon's dream team is:

1. John O'Leary
(Dublin)

2. Robbie O'Malley
(Meath)

3. Mick Lyons
(Meath)

4. Martin O'Connell
(Meath)

5. Páidí Ó Sé
(Kerry)

6. Kieran McGeeney
(Armagh)

7. Seamus Moynihan
(Kerry)

8. Jack O'Shea
(Kerry)

9. Brian Mullins
(Dublin)

10. Larry Tompkins
(Cork)

11. Greg Blaney
(Down)

12. Pat Spillane
(Kerry)

13. Colm 'Gooch' Cooper
(Kerry)

14. Peter Canavan
(Tyrone)

15. Matt Connor
(Offaly)

# The Script of Hurt

## John Maughan

The story of Mayo football over the last fifty years has been written on the script of hurt. Few people are more intimately acquainted with its dark corners than John Maughan.

Injury cut his playing career tragically short. When he retired at the age of twenty-six he had acquired an All-Ireland College medal with Carmelite College Moate, an All-Ireland Under-21 medal, a Connacht senior medal and had been an All-Star replacement.

'I had been having trouble for a while with my cruciate ligament and I suggested to the manager of the Mayo team, John O'Mahony, that I might have a procedure. John thought I had peaked too soon and thought it would be a good time for me to have it done. Things were more serious than I realised and after five operations I knew it was over. It was devastating. From the first time I had smelled the unique aroma of a county jersey, I felt very comfortable playing for Mayo and working in the army allowed me the opportunity to maximize my potential. In UCG, one of my contemporaries was Tom Carr and we trained twice a day so football was a massive thing in my life and for it to be taken away like that was very tough on me, especially as Mayo were developing into a fine team and I felt we had the potential to win an All-Ireland.'

Not a man to stand still, Maughan threw himself into coaching with various army teams. In 1990 to his great surprise he found himself, at twenty-eight years old, being offered the opportunity to manage the Clare senior football team. He famously coached them to an historic Munster final over mighty Kerry in 1992.

'It was a magical experience but I didn't fully appreciate it at the time. Clare hadn't won a Munster title since 1917 and the "Milltown Massacre" was fresh in people's minds when Kerry clocked up a score of 9-21. When I first took the job no one suggested anything about winning a Munster Championship to me. I was brought up with a very positive outlook and my main priority was to set about giving an improved performance. The Meath game in the quarter-final of the League in '92, when we nearly beat them them even though we had two men sent off, gave me an inkling as to how good we were. The one thing I emphasised very strongly afterwards was that I did not want to see any celebrations for running Meath so close. Our time with being satisfied with moral victories was over. After that game we thought we were ready to take a Munster title. We got twenty-six players together and we got a great spirit going. I wasn't worried when we missed a penalty in the Munster final – a penalty miss so early in the game has little significance. It was almost a unique performance, in the sense that all our fifteen players played to the maximum of their potential. I felt for the Kerry trainer, Micky Ned Sullivan. I was afraid he would be made a scapegoat for Kerry's performance – which he was.

'The next morning I got a phone call at seven o'clock. I spent the next four hours sitting at the bottom of the stairs answering one call after another. Then it started to sink in how big a deal it was. I got a call from the County Board and was summonsed down to Clare for a tour of the county with the team and the Cup.'

After finishing in Clare in 1994, Maughan began the first of his two terms as Mayo manager. It was the best of times. It was the worst of times. Maughan encouraged people to put bets on Mayo to win the All-Ireland in 1996. He was to learn why many a pope goes into a conclave and arrives back a cardinal.

'My proudest day was when we beat the All-Ireland champions Galway in the Connacht final in Tuam in 1999. History has shown Tuam to be a bogey team for Mayo. Beating the then All-Ireland champions Tyrone in 2004 was another high. Likewise, beating Kerry in the All-Ireland semi-final in 1996 was very sweet.

'There is no doubt the worst moment came when we surrendered a lead to allow Meath to draw with us in the 1996 All-Ireland final. I had been absolutely convinced that we were going to win. I told punters that they were safe to back us against the bookies. So that game really hurt. I was physically sick after the game. I rushed to empty myself in the cubicle and then I had to go pick the team up for the replay two weeks later. I think we did that very well.'

The replay was marred by the mêlée that saw Liam McHale sent off. Maughan has no interest in rehashing the controversy again. 'It's all water under the bridge.'

The next year saw Maughan losing another All-Ireland final but this time it was him rather than the referee who was in the firing line.

'I took a lot of flak after the game for the way we didn't replace

*Above:* At arms length: John Maughan lays down the law. *Photo:* Roscommon Champion/ *Gerard O'Loughlin.*

Dermot Flanagan directly but made a series of switches and above all, for leaving Pat Holmes on Maurice Fitzgerald. The best man to have marked Maurice would have been Kenneth Mortimer but we needed him up in the forwards. With the benefit of hindsight, we maybe should have put someone else on Maurice with ten or fifteen minutes to go but we felt then it was best to stick to our guns.'

In 2004, Mayo fans hoped it would be a case of third time lucky for Maughan but it was not to be when they were comprehensively beaten by Kerry.

'We played fantastic football to beat Tyrone in the quarter-final but after that we were a team in decline. We were lucky to beat Fermanagh in the semi-final. I stayed on for another year but we couldn't get close to a Tyrone style performance in 2005.'

Within Mayo there is a strand of opinion that wonders how Maughan could have ignored the claims of Kevin O'Neill so often for a place on his team for big games in Croke Park.

'To be honest, I was astounded at the sort of form Kevin produced for Mayo in 2006. He did often play for Mayo when I was manager but didn't play much in Croke Park because we didn't think he was good enough. I had absolutely no agenda. If I felt he was one of my best players surely I would have brought him on if I thought he could help us win an All-Ireland? I think if you asked most people close to the scene they would say I made the right call.'

An unexpected by-product of Maughan's first period in charge of Mayo was felt in Leitrim.

'We were playing Leitrim in the Connacht Championship on live TV and a fracas developed. My instinct was to stop the row developing so I ran onto the pitch but Leitrim's Gerry Flanagan floored me with a punch. He immediately became a cult hero in Leitrim! I felt really annoyed at the time because I received a suspension afterwards when all I was doing was trying to make the peace.'

Maughan also had a short time managing Fermanagh.

'I have a reputation for being a disciplinarian and there was a concerted effort on the part of a few players to get rid of me. A meeting was called and I agreed to say on for another year but on the journey home I changed my mind, because I knew things were not right, and stepped down.'

After his second coming with Mayo, Maughan took over the Roscommon job in 2005 at a time when the county's fortunes were at an all time low on and off the pitch. He immediately created controversy when he culled some of the biggest names from the squad such as Frankie Dolan and Shane Curran.

'I knew that it was a big undertaking and would be tough going. Roscommon had been managed for a few years by Tom Carr and Tommy and I were best men at each other's weddings so we're very close and I knew how ugly things had gone for him. I thought it would be a challenge and love my involvement in football so I said yes and tried to restore stability to the county after all the disasters that had gone on before. I knew that certain players in the squad had a lifestyle that was not compatible with being a county footballer. I had heard all the rumours and read reports about all the incidents like players playing pool in the nude and so on but it wasn't my job to investigate every allegation that had been made. My job was to pick the players that would best take Roscommon forward. In autumn 2007 I did bring Frankie Dolan back in to the squad but I think Frankie will concede that he is a more mature player now than he was back then.'

Maughan's controversial tenure with Roscommon came to a fractious end in 2008 after he was subject to verbal abuse from a vocal minority of county fans.

'Football management is no easy ride. When I started with Clare back in 1990, it was fun but not anymore. You keep going only because of the incredible buzz you get when you win. Abuse is now a regular part of being a county manager. Most people will recall the abuse Tommy Lyons took when he was manager of Dublin. In 2004 Mayo beat Tyrone in Omagh in a League match. It was one of those days when things went well for us but Mickey Harte got dog's abuse for having picked a close relative on the team. I had an empty feeling coming away from that match. It was an ugly day.

'You do get abuse shouted at you when you are on the sideline. I particularly recall a game when Ciaran McDonald, who has been such a great player for Mayo, was having an off day with his frees and I thought I recognised the most vocal critic's voice. Sure enough, when I turned around it was one of the most prominent Mayo supporters in Dublin. Ciaran had walked away from Mayo football for a year and a half because of the abuse his family was getting on but this guy was lacerating him. After we beat Tyrone in 2004 in the All-Ireland quarter-final that same supporter came up to me that evening and threw his arms around me. I got my own back at his hypocrisy and reminded him of the incident with Ciaran and told him exactly what I thought of him.'

Maughan's affability is temporarily abated when asked if it is true that there has been a rupture in his relationship with John O'Mahony.

'A few people have asked me that because in 2007 John O'Mahony gave an interview when he mentioned that he stopped getting phone calls from me. When you are a county manager you don't have time to be making calls to many people outside the team. John and I were managing different counties and our job was to win for them. I have been friends with Liam Sammon for twenty years but when he took over Galway I didn't embrace him on the sideline before Roscommon played Galway in the FBD league in January '08 because I was there to win a match. If I met John O'Mahony we would have a good chat but we wouldn't be going to our respective houses for tea with each other. We're not that type of people.'

Maughan enjoys the lore of stories about the great Connacht footballers. One involves his immediate predecessor as Roscommon manager, Val Daly. In the early 1990s Connacht footballers were invariably free in August and September and many took the route of weekend tourist for trans-Atlantic games.

Before their glory days of 1998, Galway were knocked out early in the Championship one year. Jackie Sammon, a famous man in the GAA in New York, rang Val Daly and asked him to travel over to line out for Connemara Gaels the following Sunday and to bring a couple of other good players with him. Daly rang around and persuaded former Galway full-forward Brian O'Donnell to travel with him. Brian had never played in a match in New York. The two lads flew out on the Friday evening and on the plane Daly briefed his colleague on how to get through the weekend. He said, 'Now Brian, they do things differently over there. It's not like at home so just enjoy the weekend, play the match and don't mind what anyone says. Whatever you do, say nothing.'

The Tribesmen enjoyed the first part of the weekend but the match went less well. At half-time the Connemara Gaels were seven points down. Jackie Sammon gave a team-talk and said, 'Ye're the most disgraceful shower I ever saw. Ye're a disgrace to the Connemara Gaels jersey. As for the big shots from over in Ireland, I'm sorry I brought ye out at all. Daly, you were hopeless and O'Donnell, you were even worse. You didn't even catch one ball.' O'Donnell forgot Daly's advice and retorted, 'Sure, how could ye play football out there? There wasn't a single blade of grass on the pitch.' Sammon turned around to him and asked, 'Did you come out here to play football or to graze?'

John Maughan selected a dream Connacht team from his own playing days:

1. Eugene Lavin
(Mayo)

| 2. Martin Carney | 3. Pat Lindsay | 4. Seamus McHugh |
|:---:|:---:|:---:|
| (Mayo) | (Roscommon) | (Galway) |
| 5. Frank Noone | 6. Tom Donnellan | 7. Danny Murray |
| (Mayo) | (Roscommon) | (Roscommon) |

8. Willie Joe Padden          9. T. J. Kilgallon
(Mayo)                              (Mayo)

| 10. Val Daly | 11. Dermot Earley | 12. Mickey Martin |
|:---:|:---:|:---:|
| (Galway) | (Roscommon) | (Leitrim) |
| 13. Tony McManus | 14. Liam Sammon | 15. Kevin McStay |
| (Roscommon) | (Galway) | (Mayo) |

Clash of the Ash

# Gort's Golden Boy

## Josie Gallagher

Inever saw any footage of the late Josie Gallagher but I was always aware of his legendary status in Galway. I decided that there was only one person I should ask for an appraisal of his career – Micheál Ó Muircheartaigh.

'In hurling, generations of great Wexford players went without winning an All-Ireland. A lot of great Galway hurlers like Josie Gallagher and Seánie Duggan never won one and, if you like, they laid the foundations for modern day hurling in Galway. They won a National League medal and a Railway Cup, which was a big deal back then.

'I think that hurling has changed a lot for the better and many of the players, and this has amazed me because generally a lot of players hang on to the theory that their own generation was the best, those that hurled maybe thirty years ago are admitting that the modern generation of hurlers are better than they were. I think that video evidence would swing you around to that view. There is a greater emphasis on skill now. In the past, the man was played more in hurling. Now, it was never as bad as football but there was a lot of holding in the old days, for example, full-backs penned into the forwards, they held onto their man when the ball came in and kept their man away from the goalie; that would all be deemed a foul nowadays. The emphasis now is on speed and skill and I think hurling is better for that. Yet Josie Gallagher was as good as any hurler I ever saw.'

Josie Gallagher died in 1998, aged 75. Shortly afterwards, I spent an evening with the late Mick Dunne, the former RTÉ GAA commentator. He paid a unique tribute to Josie:

'One of my favourite pieces of writing is "The Hurler's Prayer":

Grant me, O Lord, a hurler's skill,
With strength of arm and speed of limb,

*Preceding page:* Goalmouth Scramble: *(left to right)* Umpire Nicky Rackard watches as Seán Duggan (on his knees) and Mick Burke are on the defence against Cork's Christy Ring and Liam Dowling in the 1953 All-Ireland final.

Unerring eye for the flying ball,
And courage to match whatever befall.
May my stroke be steady and my aim be true,
My actions manly and my misses few;
No matter what way the game may go,
May I rest in friendship with every foe.
When the final whistle for me has blown,
And I stand at last before God's judgement throne,
May the great referee when He calls my name
Say, You hurled like a man, you played the game.

'Nobody embodied the spirit of "The Hurler's Prayer" better than Josie Gallagher. He always said that if you can't meet a man afterwards and shake his hand, then there is little point in playing the game.

'He never wanted to shirk anything. If you told him, "Jump over a wall" he'd say, "Which wall?" He wouldn't go around it. He would go through it. He was brilliant. Put him in a gap in the most tense situation and nothing will get to him. He was ice cool. He was a player driven not by the thought of medals or fame but by his love for the game. He lived for those moments when he could lose himself completely in the action and experience the pure joy of competition. Hurling was not primarily about beating someone else for Josie but to search out the best in yourself.'

Josie first came to prominence when he played senior club hurling at the age of fifteen. Like so many players featured in this book, his career could be summed up as 'so near and yet so far'. There is a very thin line between laughter and loss. In his thirteen-year career as a senior hurler, he experienced the heartbreak of losing three All-Ireland semi-finals by a point and another by just two points.

In 1944, against a powerful Cork side seeking a four-in-a-row at Ennis, Galway lost by 1-10 to 3-3. Josie starred against Kilkenny in the 1945 All-Ireland semi-final in Birr. Galway were completely in control of Kilkenny in the first half and led by 2-9 to 2-1 at the interval, only to lose to a late rally from the Noresiders. In 1947, both teams met at the same stage at the same venue with the exact same result. In 1951, Josie put Galway ahead with just five minutes remaining against Wexford in the All-Ireland semi-final but the men in the purple and gold snatched victory in the dying moments. In 1952, the catalogue of misery continued when Galway lost to Cork at Limerick by 1-5 to 0-6.

There was further heartbreak in 1953. This time, Galway had beaten Kilkenny in the semi-final and qualified to play the Christy-Ring-led

*Above:* A Gala Occasion: A host of Galway legends attended the award ceremony for Galway's team of the Millennium. John Gallagher (fourth from the left, back row) accepts the award on behalf of his late father Josie. Other legends include (front row from left) Seán Duggan (third), Joe McDonagh (fifth) and (back row) Sylvie Linnane (second from left), (from right) Conor Hayes (fifth), Pete Finnerty (fourth), John Connolly (third), Noel Lane (second) and Iggy Clarke (far right).

Cork side in the All-Ireland final. Galway had the game for the winning but failed to take off Mick Burke despite the obvious concussion he had suffered during the game. What made their inaction all the more inexplicable was that Burke was marking the great Christy Ring. The parallel with the 1983 football final is heightened by the bruising battle on the day and the controversy that ensued from the fact that a large section of the Galway crowd had booed Ring throughout the game and that Galway appeared to have targeted the Cork legend for 'special treatment'. As in the case in 1983 the post match celebration was affected by events on the field. A blow had been struck on Burke during the game. So incensed were five or six of the Galway players by this that they had an altercation with Ring that evening at the official reception and returned to the Cork hotel at breakfast the next morning to again vent their displeasure, albeit only using verbal means on that occasion.

Josie's widow Mary Colette [Maisy] retains a keen interest in hurling matters and speaks authoritatively on the details of his career.

'Josie's proudest moment was the Galway team that represented

Connacht in the 1947 Railway Cup and beat a Munster side that was filled with stars like Christy Ring, Jackie Power, John Keane and Tommy Doyle. After he retired, Josie became a referee and felt honoured to referee the League final in 1958. The game has changed a lot from his time but I think what would please him most today is the sight of so many children around the town here wearing Galway jerseys.'

Before he died, as Maisy recalled, Josie had been invited to select his dream hurling team by a journalist. It was:

1. Seán Duggan
(Galway)

2. Bobby Rackard    3. Nick O'Donnell    4. Jim Treacy
(Wexford)              (Tipperary)              (Kilkenny)

5. Jimmy Finn      6. Pat Stakelum      7. Jim Young
(Tipperary)          (Tipperary)             (Cork)

8. Paddy Gantley              9. Mick Ryan
(Galway)                        (Tipperary)

10. Christy Ring    11. Mick Mackey    12. Jackie Power
(Cork)                 (Limerick)            (Limerick)

13. Jimmy Doyle    14. Nick Rackard    15. Matt Nugent
(Tipperary)           (Wexford)             (Clare)

# Jeepers Keepers

## Seán Duggan

An indication of Seán Duggan's status in the game is that his understudy in Galway was Tony Reddin – Reddin later moved to Tipperary where he established himself as one of the great goalkeepers and was chosen as goalkeeper on the official team of the Millennium. The start of Duggan's career coincided with the Emergency.

'My abiding memory from the time is of travelling to Loughrea, which was twenty miles away from us. Petrol was restricted, and transport was not readily available. How would we get there? After several meetings, it was decided that we could get the use of a turf lorry and with great secrecy we all met there from the city centre at the famous Ballybrit Racecourse. It was eleven o'clock in the morning. We had several detours, trying to avoid all the official checkpoints before we arrived two miles from Loughrea town at the spot which was to be the pick-up point after the game. We walked to the field; played our game and won. As money was tight, our refreshments were scarce: sweets, biscuits, and red lemonade. When we got back to the designated spot it emerged that our illicit transport was spotted, and our turf lorry was "on the run". So we started to walk back to Galway, getting to Craughwell village tired and hungry. We replenished ourselves there, courtesy of the local orchard. Then we heard the good news that our turf lorry was the Galway side of Craughwell, up a side road. Five miles from Galway city, our turf lorry broke down. By that stage it was it was half two in the morning. Two of the lads had a friend in the area and knocked him up and we borrowed his pony and trap. Some of us leapt in and headed for home. I jumped out at the crossroads and walked into my house. At the time, there was no lock on the door and, despite the hard times, I treated myself to the luxury of a cup of tea.'

Duggan particularly enjoyed the Oireachtas final victories in 1950 and 1952. However, the 1951 National League final against New York at the Polo Grounds is his happiest memory.

'We were one point up with a few minutes to go and New York were

*Above:* The Stamp of Authority: Seán Duggan is feted with a stamp in his honour in Galway in 2002.

awarded a twenty-one-yards free. Up stepped Terry Leahy – great hurler, master scorer. My mind was very uneasy: would it be defeat all over again? Leahy bent, lifted and struck, but his shot was saved and cleared. Then the late great Josie Gallagher sealed our victory with two more points.

'To have won at home against an up-and-coming Wexford team and to win a major national trophy before thirty-thousand exiles at the Polo Grounds is still clear and vivid and pleasing and, of course, a trip to New York in 1951 – when many people never went outside their own county – was the treat of a lifetime.'

When I asked Seán about the secret of motivation he responded by telling me a parable:

'The Notre Dame American football team found that their fortunes had declined enormously and their playing standards had reached rock bottom. The school decided that the team was not worthy of wearing the traditional Notre Dame colours. For years they played in the second strip. Then a team came together and qualified for a minor final. In accordance with the custom in American football, the team went out and were introduced to the crowd. Then they went back into the dressing room for their final instruction. There, hanging on every player's peg was the traditional jersey of Notre Dame. The coach told them to throw away their old jerseys and put on the traditional colours. When the team left the dressing room they felt like kings. It's all about knowing what buttons to push and when to push them.'

Duggan pays particular tribute to one man: 'Michael O'Hehir was the man who brought hurling games in vivid form to the people of rural Ireland at a time when television was unknown and transistors unheard of. He showed that hurling is a game that is an art apart, its extent and depth perhaps not fully realised, rather merely accepted. He was a national institution. As we march, not always successfully, to the relentless demands of a faster, more superficial age, just to hear his voice was to know that all was well with the world. He painted pictures with words like a master craftsman. Young boys listening him decided immediately they wanted to join the ranks of the football and hurling immortals. Irish sport is not the same without him. He was irreplaceable.'

Seán's brother Jimmy is another of the legends of the game, as John Connolly explained to me: 'My first memory of playing for Galway is tinged with a regret. I started in 1967 and I remember being brought on for the great Jimmy Duggan at left-half-back against Clare in a Munster Hurling Championship. I always had a great respect for Jimmy. He was a gentleman on and off the field and for such a small fellow he was a mighty bit of stuff. But I had to go out that day and tell him myself that I was replacing him.'

After ten years of inter-county hurling an eye injury brought a premature end to Seán Duggan's career in 1953. By that stage 'the agility of youth was fading'. He would like to see Galway playing Championship hurling in either Leinster or Munster.

'Down the decades when Galway had some great men and very fine teams, games were lost through lack of competition. That vital edge was missing in close finishes – it cost us several games and possibly titles over the years.'

Duggan is confident about the future of Gaelic games. 'The GAA will succeed and progress as long as it has the support of people; the club is the cell of growth and renewal. Hurling is woven into Irish history. The roar of the crowds, the whirr of the flying sliotar and the unmistakable and unique sound of the ash against ash has enthralled sport fans for decades.'

Seán has a nice line in self-deprecation.

'I played minor for Galway at sixteen and spent two seasons in those ranks. In a minor semi-final against Kilkenny, Galway lost by about nine goals. After the match I overheard a Galway fan express the hope that he had "seen the last of that fellow in goal".'

Seán's prodigious talents were recognised when he was chosen on the Centenary team of greatest players never to have won an All-Ireland medal. That team was:

1. Seán Duggan
(Galway)

2. Jim Fives     3. Noel Drumgoole     4. J. J. Doyle
(Galway)     (Dublin)     (Clare)

5. Seán Herbert     6. Seán Stack     7. Colm Doran
(Limerick)     (Clare)     (Wexford)

8. Joe Salmon     9. Jobber McGrath
(Galway)     (Westmeath)

10. Josie Gallagher     11. Martin Quigley     12. Kevin Armstrong
(Galway)     (Wexford)     (Antrim)

13. Jimmy Smyth     14. Christy O'Brien     15. Mick Bermingham
(Clare)     (Laois)     (Dublin)

# Jim'll Fix It

## Jim Fives

Salthill resident Jim Fives has an unusual distinction. He played football for one county and hurling for three counties. He was chosen at right-full-back on the Centenary team of the greatest players never to have won an All-Ireland medal. While medals were few and far between, the former army officer won many representative honours. In 1953, he played for Ireland against the Universities, and the following year, when the Universities were not thought to be strong enough to field a testing opposition, Fives was chosen on the Combined Services team – made up of players from the universities, the gardaí and the army – to play Ireland. In 1959 he captained the Rest of Ireland in a prestigious fixture against All-Ireland champions Tipperary.

Fives first made his name as a forward with his club, Tourin in Waterford. Early in his career he learned that hurling was not game for softies. 'In 1948, I played a senior club match in Waterford. It was a niggly game and there was a lot of moaning to the referee, the great Limerick player, Garrett Howard. At half-time, he brought the two teams together and said, "Let's have no more of this whinging. Hurling is a man's game. It's not tennis. Be men and take your challenges and your punishment. Go back out there and play like men possessed." Nobody held back. There were some fierce challenges, and an awful lot of sore limbs the next day!'

Fives was the youngest of five brothers who all played senior hurling with their native county; Jim lined out for the county football team for two years. He made his hurling debut for Waterford against Wexford. It was a baptism of fire as his immediate opponent was no less a player than Billy Rackard. Waterford's defeat that day was an omen of things to come.

'The biggest disappointment of my time with Waterford came when we lost to Tipperary by two points in the Munster championship in 1951. They were the big power then, and we were so close. We never put it together after that.

'The Waterford team that won the All-Ireland in 1948 was a

relatively old team and they broke up straight after that win. We had a poor team while I was there. You have to remember that it's a small county and the number of clubs playing the game is small. Another problem is that we had not the right management structures. We had far too many selectors and this led to a lot of "political" selection decisions, with selectors sometimes more interested in having players from their club on the team than having the fifteen best players. Of course, that was not a problem unique to Waterford but at the time we couldn't afford to be going out with a weaker side.'

After cadet school, Fives was transferred to Renmore in Galway, and for the next four years he continued to play for Waterford even though he was playing his club football and hurling in the west. In 1955, he declared for Galway.

'It wasn't near as easy then to move around from Galway to Waterford as it is now. The hardest part was when I had to play for Galway against Waterford – in the All-Ireland semi-final in 1957 and in 1959. We played them in the Munster championship because Galway were "in Munster" then. It was a very, very difficult thing to play against your native county.'

As had been the case with Waterford, Fives played for Galway during lean times. The highlight was winning the Oireachtas final by a big score over Wexford in 1958. They also enjoyed some good performances in the Railway Cup, notably a draw with Munster in 1957 and a victory over Leinster in the 1959 semi-final, although Munster beat them in the final in the newly renovated Croke Park.

Fives also hurled in Africa. He served on two UN peacekeeping missions, spending six months in both the Congo and the Middle East.

'It was very interesting, but very demanding and tense,' he recalls. 'The soldiers played hurling during their free time. The kindest thing I can say about our pitches is that they were very dusty!'

A serious back injury caused him to step down from senior inter-county hurling in 1959 but two years later, he was transferred to Castlerea and came out of retirement to play junior hurling for Roscommon. In 1964, Fives was transferred once more, and had hardly arrived at his new posting in Castlebar when he was asked if he would play for Mayo the following Sunday. The old back injury had returned, however, and Fives was forced to decline the offer.

Fives' move to Galway coincided with a switch from playing in the forwards to the backs. 'I was anxious to play in the backs because I always like to be facing the ball. The thing about forward play is that you always have to turn once you get possession.'

*Above:* The pride of the parish: Jim Fives says the obligatory 'few words' at a club function at the famous Liam Mellows Hurling Club in Galway in 2000.

He has mixed feelings about developments in the game of hurling since his playing days.

'The game is very fast now, which is a great thing. However, I'm a little disappointed that there is so little emphasis on ground hurling and also so little overhead hurling. It's almost as if catching the ball has become everything. I also think too much allowance is made for the player in possession, especially the way they are allowed to take too many steps.'

He has fond memories of one famous opponent.

'My favourite character in the game was Kilkenny's "Diamond" Hayden. At the time, there wasn't much contact between players from the different counties as there is now, but in 1951 we went with Kilkenny to London, so I got to know Diamond then. He was a great believer in psychological warfare. He would do everything and anything to put you off your game. He was always talking himself up, always trying to get you to think that you would be much better off trying to find someone else to mark.

'I believe Christy Ring played those sort of mind games as well though he never did on me. He probably felt that he didn't need to. Ring was the best player I ever saw. I marked him in Railway Cup matches. It was a very trying experience as a back because, not alone did you never know what he was going to do, a lot of the time you never knew where he was! He just ghosted into positions. One minute you were right beside him – the next he was gone and you were left for dead!'

Fives began his dream team selection with Tony Reddin, the legendary Tipperary goalkeeper who became part of hurling folklore after an altercation with Cork player and politician, Jack Lynch. During the white heat of a Cork versus Tipperary clash, Lynch charged into Reddin and, in the process, bundled both of them into the net. Reddin had something of a speech impediment but still managed to roar: 'F-f-f-f\*\*k you, Lynch. Try that again an' there'll be a f-f-f-\*\*king by-election.'

Fives' ideal team from the hurlers of his era is:

1. Tony Reddin
(Tipperary)

2. Bobby Rackard    3. Nick O'Donnell    4. Jimmy Brohan
(Wexford)              (Wexford)               (Cork)

5. Seamie Cleere    6. John Keane       7. Iggy Clarke
(Kilkenny)            (Waterford)             (Galway)

8. Joe Salmon                9. Jack Lynch
(Galway)                      (Cork)

10. Josie Gallagher   11. Mick Mackey    12. Christy Ring
(Galway)               (Limerick)             (Cork)

13. Paddy Kenny      14. Nick Rackard    15. Jimmy Smyth
(Tipperary)            (Wexford)              (Clare)

# Galway Boys' Hurrah

## Iggy Clarke

Iggy Clarke laughs heartily when I quote Antrim's Sambo McNaughton's comment to him: 'My innocent perception of the priesthood changed when I first marked Fr Iggy Clarke.' He confesses with a mischevious grin: 'He was probably right. The hurling field is no place for holiness!'

Clarke was part of the beginning of a new era in Galway hurling, when he captained the county to their first All-Ireland Under-21 title against Dublin in 1972. Three years later, a National League medal came to Clarke.

'The watershed and one of my hurling highlights was beating Tipperary in that final for, in those days, the blue and gold jersey of Tipp had for us a hue of invincibility attached to it.'

There was disappointment, though, later that year when Galway lost the All-Ireland final to Kilkenny.

'We beat Cork by two points in the '75 semi-final. After that, the euphoria in Galway was unbelievable. The county was on a roller-coaster.

But the expectations weren't based on reality. We were still not ready to face a team of the calibre of Kilkenny and learned that in the final.

'The following year we were a more potent force. We drew with Wexford in a great semi-final game and lost the replay by a goal. It was an extremely hot summer. The two games were played within a week of each other and the replay was within two weeks of the All-Ireland final. The game burned a lot of stamina. I believe if either ourselves or Wexford had won the first day, that Cork would have been defeated in the final.'

In 1979 Clarke had been ordained when Galway played Kilkenny again in the final. The Westerners made a present of two soft goals to the men in amber and black.

'We wasted a lot in the first half. I don't think the rain suited us. Kilkenny were spurred on by the defeat at the hands of Cork the previous year and didn't want a second successive defeat. There is a photograph as I'm walking off the field disconsolate and downhearted and Eddie Keher saying to me: "You'll be there again next year." But I was not even looking at him. I was just thinking to myself that we could have and should have won that game.'

Unfortunately, injury prevented Clarke from lining out in Galway's historic All-Ireland triumph over Limerick in 1980. His contribution was publicly acknowledged by Joe Connolly during his tour de force acceptance speech.

'In the All-Ireland semi-final against Offaly I was flying it. A high ball came in falling between the half-back and full-back line which I

*Left:* Tougher than the rest: Iggy Clarke breaks out of defence to launch another Galway attack.

*Facing page:* Bless Me Father: Iggy Clarke has a word with the late President Paddy Hillery during the 1980 All-Ireland final between Galway and Limerick.

*Above:* Hip hip hooray: Iggy Clarke raises the Liam McCarthy Cup after the 1980 All-Ireland defeat of Limerick.

retreated to gather. I gained possession from Mark Corrigan and dodged his tackle. Out of the corner of my eye, I saw Padraig Horan coming to tackle me and I avoided him but I failed to see Johnny Flaherty, whose tackle from behind drove up my shoulder blade and broke the clavicle. As I went down, I could feel the heat of the rush of blood. I knew I was in trouble. I waited for the free that never came. Seán Silke was behind me saying, "Iggy let go of the ball." I opened my hand and he cleared it down the field. I was removed on a stretcher and faintly heard the applause of the crowd in my ears but in my mind, I clearly saw my prospects of playing in the All-Ireland disappearing fast.

'The pain was unreal. I was placed against the X-ray machine in the Mater Hospital and I was afraid I was going to faint. A nurse tried to take off my jersey but it was agony so I told her: "For God's sake, cut it off." I suppose I kept half-hoping, for a while, that I might be back for the final but it was not realistic.

'During the second half of the All-Ireland I came out from the dugout and went up to the Hogan Stand. I had to mind my shoulder and didn't want to be crushed by people at the presentation. I had an inner feeling, you might say a premonition, that the lads were going to win even

*Above:* The eyes have it: Iggy Clarke (right) watches the toss of the coin before the 1977 All-Ireland semi-final against Cork.

though the game wasn't over. On the way, people kept asking me if we were going to win and if I was praying. After his wonderful speech, Joe Connolly handed me the cup, which enabled me to feel part of the whole victory. It was such a beautiful moment to hold it up in front of the crowd. We all felt that we were part of a turning point, a special moment in hurling history when Galway would take its rightful place at hurling's top table.'

There was further disappointment for Clarke in 1981.

'We were coasting in the All-Ireland final at half-time despite John Connolly's disallowed goal. We looked like winning until Johnny Flaherty's goal and even then I thought we were good enough to come back. It was a bitter pill to lose but the defeat didn't hurt me as much as '79. That year, we hadn't won an All-Ireland and I was very aware of the so-called curse on Galway hurlers which said we would never win an All-Ireland. As a priest, I wanted to disprove that rubbish and we had achieved that in 1980.'

He retired at the tender age of thirty-two in the GAA's Centenary Year, having won four All-Star awards. 'At that stage I didn't have the passion for it any longer.'

In 1997, Clarke left the priesthood and is now married to Marie. He works as a deputy principal in a school in Galway and as a professional counsellor on a part-time basis. However, it was his experiences in the priesthood that provided him with his most amusing memory from his career.

'The morning of the All-Ireland final in 1981, I was saying Mass for the team in the hotel. The gospel that day was about the parable of the mustard seed: the smallest grows into the biggest seed. In my sermon, I gave a very eloquent philosophical presentation on how the story of the mustard seed equated with our journey as a team. In '75 we were a tiny seed but in '81 it would really go into fruition. That night at the meal we were all down because we felt we had left another All-Ireland behind us. Joe Connolly turned to me and said: "Jaysus whatever happened to that mustard seed?!"'

The dream team that Clarke would have liked to have played on features players from his playing days:

1. Noel Skehan
(Kilkenny)

2. Fan Larkin       3. Pat Hartigan       4. John Horgan
(Kilkenny)             (Limerick)              (Cork)

5. Joe McDonagh     6. Seán Silke       7. Iggy Clarke
(Galway)               (Galway)               (Galway)

8. John Connolly       9. Frank Cummins
(Galway)                 (Kilkenny)

10. Jimmy Barry Murphy     11. Pat Delaney       12. Martin Quigley
(Cork)                     (Kilkenny)              (Wexford)

13. Noel Lane       14. Ray Cummins       15. Eddie Keher
(Galway)               (Cork)                (Kilkenny)

(Note: Iggy is the only player put together his dream in this way.)

# In the Fast Lane

## Noel Lane

The first sign Noel Lane received that he had potential as a hurler came in national school when any time a new batch of hurleys came to the school 'the Master' gave him first pick. At secondary school, he played at wing-back but because he used his left hand on top of the hurley the priest in charge of the team told him he would not be selected until he used his right on top. The transition did not come easily and years later, when he started playing for Galway, he was still switching hands.

As a child he was reared on a diet of football and his heroes were the legends of Galway's three-in-a-row side. To this day he is friends with the goalkeeper on that team, Johnny Geraghty. His hurling career really took off when he began his career with the Department of Forestry. While he was based in Offaly, he found himself with spare time in abundance. At school, the focus had been on the skills of the game but he learned that there was more to the beautiful game than just beauty. He decided to train with the local team in Kinnity where he lined out against Johnny Flaherty and Pat Delaney. The matches took place with no lines on the pitch, generally in near darkness and with no referee. They were all games to stand up and be counted in – especially in Lane's case as his regular opponent was Offaly's Mick Cleere, a man known for his ferocious commitment. 'It was all part of the steeling process.'

The benefits of his new education were soon evident when he played club hurling in Ballinderreen with Joe McDonagh. The team reached the county semi-final in 1977 and the county final in '78. His club form was rewarded with a call-up to the county panel for the 1977–78 League campaign, and he made his debut against Clare in Tulla. His build-up to the game was unusual.

'I was over-awed going into the dressing room with all my heroes from the National League win in 1975. There was some great characters like John Connolly and Joe McDonagh who went out of their way to give me confidence. P. J. Molloy was preparing for the game by rubbing poitín

on to his legs. Poitín was hard enough to get at the time so it didn't seem a good use of it to me. I asked him for the bottle and said: "Better value to slug it than to rub it." So I had a sup. It didn't do me any harm. I was marking Johnny McMahon who was an All-Star and I was thrilled with my performance. I held my place after that.'

A shake-up of the team was necessary after they suffered a heavy defeat to Tipperary in the 1979 National League final. Lane was one of the casualties and was dropped from the panel. Breaking the news sensitively to him was not a priority for the Galway management.

'I got a letter in an envelope which was handed to me in the dressing room in a club game. I smelled a rat. No reason was giving for my omission. It was just: "We regret to inform you . . ." I felt it was severe to drop me like that.'

The opportunity for redemption came quickly. Galway were unimpressive in the All-Ireland quarter-final against Laois that year. Niall McInerney was put at full-forward as an experiment but it had not worked well.

'Babs Keating was training Galway at the time. He spearheaded a delegation that came down to see me to ask me back. I replied: "Not a chance." I was just playing hard to get. I was the first one in Athenry for training that evening.

'Babs was an excellent manager. As I was moved into full-forward,

*Left:* Musical Lanes: Noel Lane and Sylvie Linnane rock and roll as they audition for a place in Bruce Springsteen's band as Galway celebrate their All-Ireland triumph in 1987.

*Facing page:* The First Noel: Before the 1986 All-Ireland final, Noel Lane introduces the Galway team to GAA president Mick Loftus (second from left) and President Patrick Hillery who shakes hands with Gerry McInerney. Pete Finnerty (sixth from right) looks on with wry amusement.

he gave me a lot of his time and attention coaching me on how to approach forward play and working on my solo and my passing. He gave me a lot of confidence in my own game. I really admired him as a player for Tipp. We had thought of ourselves as inferior to the big powers like Cork and Tipperary but he was one of them and I suppose to our surprise he was a normal guy. He gave us a lot of confidence. Babs was "let go" after we lost the 1979 All-Ireland but I believe the belief he gave us was a significant factor in our breakthrough the following year.'

Lane also has a high opinion of Keating's successor. 'Cyril Farrell was a brilliant manager. His talent was shown especially in the way he managed players who were that bit more difficult to manage like Tony Keady and Brendan Lynskey. Cyril had great man-management skills.'

One incident illustrates this capacity. The week before the 1988 All-Ireland final the team was training in Ballinasloe on the night the line-up was due to be announced for the final. There was a terrible storm that evening with thunder, lightning and incredible rain. Lynskey and Keady did not travel down from Dublin. Farrell felt like cutting the two miscreants from the team but knew he could not win the final without them. Things were tense for a while especially as he never picked a team until the squad was there to hear it first. He arranged a training session for the next evening and this time the two stars were back and victory was secured.

'Cyril always preached we were better than everybody else. He had great passion and would get us to see the opposition in terms of what they didn't have more than what they did have. He inherited Babs' team in '79 but really showed his skills with his "second team" from 1985-90. He would have worked with most of that team at Minor and Under-21. He knew everything about them: what they ate and drank, who they slept with and their strengths and weaknesses.'

Lane's first All-Ireland came in 1980.

'We won that day because our leaders, especially Joe Connolly, stood up and were counted. We were a powerful team and that side should have won more than one All-Ireland. It suited us that day that we were playing Limerick rather than Cork or Kilkenny and that gave us confidence. It felt like it was for us that day, though Limerick could have considered themselves unlucky.

'It was a proud time to be from Galway but I don't know were we ready for the celebrations that came afterwards. For six months afterwards, we were touring schools and clubs. Every night we could have been out if we wanted to. I was very lucky in that my wife Carmel kept me on the straight and narrow and gave me great support in the low points of my career and that my daughter Aoife was born that year. Likewise, my sons Mark and Patrick helped me to keep my focus. All that 1980 team were very lucky in that respect also. I can't give enough credit to the wives and partners who supported us but I can understand how that kind of absence from home has destroyed relationships and marriages for some players on other teams.'

Galway's triumph that year created one of the funniest memories from Lane's time with Galway.

'We went to America on the All-Star trip and brought a big contingent of Galway supporters with us. We visited Disneyland and a gang of us went on the Space Mountain Train ride. I was sharing a carriage with Steve Mahon and some of the lads like Finbarr Gantley were behind us. Two of the most "mature" members of the group, John Connolly's dad, Pat, and Mick Sylver were behind them. After we came down we were all petrified and just glad to have got out of there alive. We went to a little bar nearby to catch our breaths back. Just as we started to relax who did we see in the queue to go back up Space Mountain but Pat and Mick!

'On that trip and the ones I went afterwards when I won my two All-Stars (in '83 and '84) or all the times I went as replacements I became very good friends with the Kerry lads. They were there every year. They were really fond of Galway hurlers but not near as fond of the Galway footballers! I think it went back to the 1960s when Galway beat them too often for their liking.'

After the disappointment of losing the All-Ireland 1981 final to Offaly, Galway had some lean years. Things took a turn for the better in 1985.

'We had a new side that year with just a few survivors of the 1980 team. We got great new players in, notably a wonderful half-back line. We beat the All-Ireland champions Cork in the semi-final. It was a wet day and there was surface water on the pitch but we caught fire. We were always capable of doing that in a semi-final. Our problem was maintaining that right through to a final and we lost to Offaly that year. In '86 we beat Kilkenny in the semi-final. Joe Cooney really came of age that day. Cyril used a two-man full-forward line for that game and it worked a treat. We were good enough to win in '86 but tactically we got it wrong. We repeated the two-man full-forward line in the final but it shattered our confidence when it didn't work and Cork grew in confidence and won.'

Lane felt the pain of that defeat in a very personal way.

'I was captain that year. We won the Railway Cup that year but lost the finals of the Oireachtas tournament, the National League and the All-Ireland. Personally, I didn't have a good game in the All-Ireland and found the whole experience very disappointing.

'The night before the All-Ireland I couldn't sleep, which didn't help me in Croke Park. I felt the pressure as captain and was really keen to do well. When you are young, you don't suffer from nerves as much. Back in 1979 I had got a full eight hours' sleep the night before the final but on the morning of the match I met Frank Burke and John Connolly and they had slept so badly that they decided to go for a walk down the streets of Dublin at three or four in the morning. I thought they were crazy then but I understood in '86. The one thing I sometimes worry about is when I see panelists on TV almost character assassinating players not realising the number of reasons why a player may underperform on the big stage.'

The disappointment of '86 took its toll on Lane.

'My form suffered after that and I was lucky to be on the panel in '87. I came on as a sub in the All-Ireland semi-final in '87. I felt very nervous coming on to the pitch and I was wondering to myself: what am I doing here? Then I got a goal and it lifted the weight of the previous year off my shoulders. I came on as a sub in the final against Kilkenny and scored another goal. It might have been the worst goal ever scored in Croke Park but it still counted!

'In '88 I was back starting on the team but after scoring 1-5 in the All-Ireland semi-final to my amazement and disgust I was dropped for the final on the Tuesday night before the game. I hadn't seen it coming. I let Cyril know my feelings on the subject in no uncertain terms and in

*Above:* It's now or never: Noel Lane leads the Galway team before the 1986 All-Ireland final.

choice language. I left Ballinasloe in a hurry and went home feeling sorry for myself and believing an injustice had been done to me. I proceeded to Loughrea and drank twelve pints of beer. On the Thursday night, realising that I was lucky to be there at all, I went up to Cyril and said: "You heard what I did in Loughrea and you heard what I said to you on Tuesday night but if you want me Sunday I'll be there."

'I came on after half-time. It was one of the great All-Irelands. There was great rivalry and great duels. One of the decisive factors was that our full-back Conor Hayes had Nicky English in his grip. If they had moved English we would have been in trouble. I think the captaincy played on Nicky. I got in around the square and scored a goal that was instrumental in us getting the result.

'I was injured in '89 with back problems. I felt we should have won the three-in-a-row because we had a substantially better team than Tipperary and we had broken their spirit the previous two years. I felt we allowed ourselves to be distracted by the Keady affair. We should have just got on with it. There was a belief in Galway that the powers that be were out to get us. Evidence to support that belief came when Sylvie was sent off for an innocuous enough challenge. Sylvie's fiery play often drew attention to him but that day it was a very harsh sending off and then Hopper McGrath was sent off as well. We were missing key players that year due to injury.

'In '90 I was back in the starting line-up for the final against Cork. I was thirty-six then and might have been better off used as an impact sub. We had a good lead but the turning point came when Martin Naughton had a shot for goal but it was deflected and we didn't get a sixty-five. Instead they got a goal from the puck-out and then another one immediately afterwards. Instead of us getting a goal, they got two. We could and should have won that final. We took wrong options and our defence was torn apart in the second half. It would be wrong to blame them, though, as we missed great chances in the forwards. I think, had we won in '89, we would have won in '90 because after losing against Tipp, doubts set in. I felt we also made a mistake by letting Sylvie and Conor Hayes go. Had they been there, Cork would have not got all the goals they did.'

1991 saw Lane's swansong in the Galway jersey. 'I was brought on as a sub in the semi-final against Tipperary but I had no impact on the game. My time was over.'

Lane returned to prominence again when he controversially became manager of the Galway senior team, having served his apprenticeship at club level and with the county minors and Under-21s. It is quickly evident that he still feels aggrieved by the manner of his treatment by the county board. Things began promisingly for Lane when Galway beat Kilkenny in the 2001 All-Ireland semi-final.

'I succeeded Mattie Murphy whether it was right or wrong. He was doing a good job but was only given two years. I believe that Galway should have won one or two All-Irelands in the last ten years because the team was good enough but there was a lack of continuity at management level. The players were the ones to suffer.

'Beating Kilkenny was a win against the head and one of the highs in my life because I had prepared a team to beat the best but I knew that the knives were out for me at the County Board level even when we won for reasons unknown to me. It was fed back indirectly to me that the County Board was not supporting me. Things had deteriorated after a League match in Tipperary. It was blatantly obvious that I was not acting as they wanted. I was doing things that I felt would help us to win, like flying the team to Croke Park for games. As manager, I had taken control of the team and I don't think that pleased them. I brought in Mike McNamara from Clare. He was a great trainer and was very good on mental toughness and mental preparation.

'The lack of support from the County Board took its toll on me in the lead-up to the All-Ireland final against Tipperary. I had a huge management job outside the players with media commitments and everything else. If I got the chance again I would do things differently and put more focus on the players alone. By contrast Nicky English, the Tipp manager, had been in the job for four or five years so he had that experience to call on. The referee made some astonishing decisions that day which I felt cost us. As the co-operation from the County Board wasn't there I had to take on all the organisational details myself. I was emotionally and physically drained from the whole management of the weekend which I think meant that I didn't react sharply enough to events on the sideline during the game and in that respect I feel I let down the players. I lost five All-Irelands as a player but losing as a manager was worse because I felt responsible for thirty people in the squad and the back-room team. I knew straight away that the knives were out again.

'The next year we beat Cork in the quarter-final in Thurles so I must have been doing something right. We played Clare in the semi-final in a very tight and intense game. Clare sucked us in and played the game on their terms. Colin Lynch floated a typical point to snatch the victory for them. That was when I knew the show was over. The press knew. There were long smiles on many of the County Board. I felt I was just growing into the job and would have benefited from another year or two but it was very hurtful to effectively be sacked.'

Lane's dream team of players of recent vintage, excluding Galway players, is:

1. Damien Fitzhenry
(Wexford)

2. Tommy Walsh     3. Brian Lohan     4. Brian Corcoran
(Kilkenny)        (Clare)        (Cork)

5. Brian Whelahan     6. Seán McMahon     7. Ken McGrath
(Offaly)        (Clare)        (Waterford)

8. Joe Hennessey        9. Ciarán Carey
(Kilkenny)        (Limerick)

10. Johnny Dooley     11. Martin Storey     12. Henry Shefflin
(Offaly)        (Kilkenny)        (Kilkenny)

13. Nicky English     14. D. J. Carey     15. Eoin Kelly
(Tipperary)        (Kilkenny)        (Tipperary)

# Sleeping Beauty

## Sylvie Linnane

The most famous quote in the hurling vernacular is Micheál Ó Muircheartaigh's observation: 'A mighty poc from the hurl of Seán Óg Ó hAlpín . . . his father was from Fermanagh, his mother from Fiji, neither a hurling stronghold.'

However, a good contender for runner–up must be, 'Sylvie Linnane: the man who drives a JCB on a Monday and turns into one on a Sunday.' Of all the interviews for this book, the most revealing comment came from the mouth of Linnane: 'I would rather be taken off than sent off.'

His fire-and-brimstone approach to the game often concealed his innate talent, though winning three All-Star awards does indicate his craftsmanship. He won five Railway Cup medals and two National Leagues. However, it was the contests rather than the medals that meant the most to Sylvie. 'For me the colour of a jersey, especially the Kilkenny one, was all I needed to get up for a game. I always had a passion for beating them. Everyone likes to take their scalp. I was never one to say anything to an opponent but I did believe they should know I was there. One time we were playing Kilkenny, I received an uppercut from Harry Ryan before the National Anthem. I couldn't see after it but I still let fly at him.

'The other thing I remember was the incredible reception we got when we won the All-Ireland in 1980. It was clear how much it meant to people. The great thing was they were all there again when we lost the next year.'

Linnane lined out at right-half-back on the Galway team that won the breakthrough All-Ireland in 1980 and at right-full-back when Galway won All-Irelands in 1987 and '88. Of the four All-Irelands he lost the one that wounded most was the defeat to Offaly in 1981. 'We shot fourteen wides in the second half. You can't afford that.'

Sylvie gives a nuanced reply when asked about the team's coach, Cyril Farrell.

'Cyril was great to motivate a team before a big match. In '87 in the All-Ireland semi-final we were up against Tipperary. When they won the Munster final their captain Richie Staklelum said: "The famine is over". That was the motivation he used to beat them. We had lost All-Ireland finals in '85 and '86 and there was no way we were going to lose three in a row although Kilkenny really put it up to us in a tough match. The problem with Cyril was that he wasn't quick enough to make changes on the sideline when we were losing in Croke Park, especially in All-Ireland finals.'

Inevitably, in a discussion of Galway hurling in the 1980s the name of Tony Keady features prominently.

'The '88 final as a unit was one of our best games. It was very close until Noel Lane came on and scored a late goal. The Sunday Game had cameras live at our celebratory dinner and there was a dramatic hush when Ger Canning announced on live television: "And now the moment you have all been waiting for. The Sunday Game Man of the match is . . . Tony Keady." Suddenly everybody started around but there was no sign of Tony. We found out later that he was five miles away in a pub with Brendan Lynskey and their friends.

'Tony was Texaco hurler of the year that year. That was why he was such a big loss to us the following year with the infamous "Keady affair".

*Below:* The Clash of the Ash: Sylvie Linnane competes for the ball with no thought for his safety during the 1987 All-Ireland final against Kilkenny.

After he was suspended for a year there was an appeal but he lost twenty to eighteen. Seán Tracey came in for him and he did well for us but we weren't the same tight unit of six backs as we had been when he was there. Nothing would have come through the middle with him there and he would have scored two or three points from long-range frees as he always did. Before the game and the appeal there was a lot of discussion about whether Tony would play and that was very distracting for us. Our focus was not as good as it should have been for a team seeking three in a row. In the game itself there were a lot of decisions given against us. Somebody made a comment afterwards about the referee: "He was either biased against us or he was a sh*te referee." Pete Finnerty said he was both.

'I think we all felt angry about the Keady affair because there were hundreds of footballers and hurlers going to play in America at the time but Tony was the one that was made a scapegoat of. Keady says that when he dies, he wants the words on his tombstone to be: "He should have played in '89!"

Cyril Farrell revealed an enterprising side to Linnane's character: 'Sylvie loved a nice hurley. He always travelled to training with Seán Silke. Silke and Iggy Clarke used get the hurls for us. Silke would usually have

*Below:* Rearguard action: Sylvie Linnane leads the Galway defence in a vanguard action against Limerick in the 1980 All-Ireland final.

*Above:* Don't mess with me! Sylvie Linnane strikes a typically defiant pose in the build-up to the 1988 All-Ireland final. *Photo:* Irish Examiner

hurls in his boot. When Sylvie needed a hurl he would get out of the car as Seán left him home after training to get his gear and sneak off with the hurl he liked most. The next day Seán would ask him if he took the hurl. Sylvie would always deny it point blank. Then a few weeks later he would casually stroll into training with the missing hurl!'

Linnane laughs when it is suggested that the title of Graham Geraghty's book *Misunderstood* might apply to him also. He has spent half a lifetime denying some of the dramas attributed to him on the pitch. However, it is a little known fact that he once created a drama off the pitch.

'We were in Dublin the night before an All-Ireland final and, as always, we were sent to bed early. The problem is that it's very hard to sleep the night before an All-Ireland. I was rooming with Steve Mahon and we heard a massive row going on in the street underneath. So I went to investigate and saw this fella beating up his wife or his girlfriend. I ran into the bathroom, got the waste-paper basket, filled it with water and ran over to the window and threw the water over the man. It did the trick and he stopped and the woman ran away. A happy ending or so I thought until the man recovered from the shock and got really, really angry and started to climb up the drain-pipe to pay back the person who threw the water on him. I didn't think the night before the All-Ireland was the best time to get involved in a brawl – especially as this guy looked like a pure psycho and I decided discretion was the better part of valour. I turned off the light so he wouldn't know where to find me. I went quietly back to bed and listened attentively to see what would happen. What I hadn't known at the time was that the light immediately below my room was on! The room belonged to the former Galway great Inky Flaherty. Inky was not a man to mess with and a few minutes later I heard him forcefully eject the intruder out the window – which was not the typical way to prepare for an All-Ireland.'

The ever-helpful side of Sylvie's nature was also revealed shortly before the end of the 1988 All-Ireland when Nicky English asked: 'How much time left, ref?'

Linnane quickly interjected: 'At least another year for Tipperary!'

Sylvie's dream team is:

1. Ger Cunningham
(Cork)

2. Brian Murphy          3. Conor Hayes          4. Joe Hennessey
(Cork)                    (Galway)                 (Kilkenny)

5. Pete Finnerty         6. Ger Henderson         7. Anthony Daly
(Galway)                  (Kilkenny)               (Clare)

8. Frank Cummins                    9. John Connolly
(Kilkenny)                           (Galway)

10. Nicky English        11. John Power           12. Joe Connolly
(Tipperary)               (Kilkenny)               (Galway)

13. Pat Fox              14. Noel Lane            15. D. J. Carey
(Tipperary)              (Galway)                 (Kilkenny)

We Could Be Heroes

# Alan Kerins and John Tiernan

This chapter brings together the stories of two extraordinary young men – linked by a common desire to make a difference.

## *Out of Africa*

Given the demands on the modern player, the dual star is increasingly rendered an endangered species. In 2001, Alan Kerins was on the verge of making history but his hopes of becoming a dual All-Ireland winner in the one year were thwarted when Tipperary beat the Westerners in the hurling final. He did have the consolation, though, of coming off the bench to help the Galway footballers claim their second All-Ireland under the stewardship of John O'Mahony. It was real Roy of the Rovers stuff.

'I had not been known for my football ability until Johnno elevated me from nowhere to a place on the Galway team. There was a very specific background to my call-up. For much of the '80s and '90s Connacht football was in the doldrums. The nadir was probably the trouncing Cork gave Mayo in the 1993 All-Ireland semi-final. So to take back the Sam Maguire trophy west to the Shannon for the first time in thirty-two years meant so much to so many and the Galway squad were very aware of that. The memory of the celebrations will live with me forever. After we won in the All-Ireland final in 1998 Galway people wanted a second All-Ireland. Yet that did not look likely in 2001 when Roscommon hammered us in the Connacht Championship. Thankfully the backdoor was introduced and we got a second chance. John knew after the Roscommon game that some radical surgery was needed to the team and I was brought on. John had the ability to put Humpty-Dumpty back together. Being together as a team is ultimately more important than winning. If a side is not together as a team, success will be transitory but if a side achieves togetherness and unity of purpose, success will follow. Johnno was able to do that.'

There were some tensions in the camp when John and Michael Donnellan threatened to walk away from the panel. Kerins deals with this

*Preceding page:* Hurling forward: Alan Kerins takes command during the All-Ireland semi-final on 21 August 2005, leaving Kilkenny's Tommy Walsh in his wake.

*Above:* The races of Castlebar: Alan Kerins helps Galway to a narrow win over old rivals Mayo in Castlebar in the 2002 Connacht Championship on 2 June.

controversy with characteristic diplomacy:

'It is striking to contrast John O'Mahony's handling of the potential landmine of the Donnellan situation with Mick McCarthy's handling of the Roy Keane situation twelve months later as Ireland's World Cup hopes threatened to implode. It really says a lot about his man-management skills.'

A good team wins an All-Ireland but it takes a great one to win a second All-Ireland. O'Mahony's Galway team achieved that against the raging hot favourites, Meath, in 2001.

'Meath had demolished Kerry in the All-Ireland semi-final and we had been beaten by Roscommon in the Connacht Championship. At that stage people thought we were dead and buried but we had a great team and we came back. I would like to think there is a lesson there for everyone. It is not about the setbacks you confront in life that matters but the key question

*Above:* Out of Africa: Alan Kerins is greeted by young friends in Zambia in 2007.
*Photo:* Damien Eagers

is how you cope with these setbacks. On a personal level, having featured in the earlier games it was disappointing to be on the bench for the start of the All-Ireland final but it was great to come on and be part of such a momentous occasion.'

It was not all smooth sailing for Kerins. He was dropped by hurling manager, Noel Lane, because he was unable to give a full commitment to the hurling team.

'Again I was disappointed because I was doing all I could to balance the two codes and John O'Mahony was doing everything in his power to make it work for me but I suppose Noel was under great pressure to win an All-Ireland and he felt it had to be an all or nothing situation. But that's all water under the bridge now.'

With the appointment of Ger Loughnane as Galway manager in 2006 fans hoped that the hurling All-Ireland would be making a welcome return west of the Shannon. However, 2007 saw a whole series of controversies with Loughnane in the centre but no titles. With John Lee, Kerins was one of the few bright sparks on the Galway team that year and he was considered unlucky not to win an All-Star award. He jokes: 'The one thing that you can be sure of when Ger is around is that things will never be boring for long!' 2008, though, was equally barren for Galway.

Away from Gaelic games, Kerins was cultivating another life. It was not for his achievements on the field of the play that led to Kerins receiving a prestigious Rehab Person of the Year award live on RTÉ television.

His new departure began in January 2005 when he took a three-month unpaid leave of absence from his job as a physiotherapist to begin work on an outreach programme with the Presentation Sisters in Mongu. Mongu is in the main township of the Western Province in Zambia, on the edge of the Kalahari Desert and the poorest region of the country – seven out of eleven million Zambians survive on just seventy-four cents a day. The experience he had in Zambia completely changed Kerins' life. His initial plan had been to continue working with the disabled but the extreme deprivation he witnessed compelled him to do more. When he returned from Ireland he set about the task of serious fund-raising and linked up with the local Cheshire Home in Mongu. The home, run by Sr Cathy Crawford, a native of Laois, is the one facility that caters for disabled children in an area that is two and a half times the size of Ireland.

Kerins founded a charity, the Alan Kerins African Projects, setting up funds for a famine-relief project – an irrigation programme to bore holes for water – as well as providing physiotherapy and prosthetic limbs for the disabled. In 2004, Zambia suffered its worst drought in seventy-seven years and around Mongu, the Cheshire Home delivered supplies to the elderly and those who had no access to food. Today it is the money from Kerins' fundraising that keeps the project alive. His charity work to date has raised in excess of €300,000 and he has helped nearly 10,000 people.

Alan Kerins came face to face in Zambia with one of the most compelling challenges to our world imaginable. The emergence of any new disease inevitably provokes fear; however, the rapid spread of AIDS, its transmissible nature and the medical complexity have exacerbated the normal problems and tensions. Kerins got the opportunity to engage with the subject in an emotionally significant and humanising way in Zambia. It was a decisive moment for him personally: 'It was probably the best thing I've ever done but, no question, it was the most difficult thing I had ever done. It had a huge effect on me. The first day I was there I saw people who were in the last stages of AIDS, and were dying. I had very rarely seen anyone dying, let alone dying from AIDS. It's a horrific way to die.'

Notwithstanding his commitment to the charity, he reassured Galway's hurling manager Ger Loughnane that he was fully dedicated to playing his part in Galway's quest to make a bold claim for an All-Ireland triumph. He hopes he will finally be able to put the disappointment of losing the All-Ireland hurling final in 2001 behind him in the most effective way possible – by winning the Liam McCarthy Cup. His experiences in Zambia have made Kerins more philosophical about sporting disappointments:

'Missing out on the All-Ireland hurling final in 2001 was probably the low point. Yet at the same time I did not allow myself to get shattered by the whole thing. I had to go on with my life.'

What, then, is it that drives Alan Kerins to continue with his work in Zambia? In the final scene of the medieval epic La Chanson de Roland the great Christian hero Charlemagne sat exhausted in Aix, his battles with the Moors over. According to the poem, he was more than 900 years old. An angel wakened the old man from his sleep and told him to get up again and return to battle because the work would not be finished until the end of time. Charlemagne sighed: 'Dieu, si penuse est ma vie.' ('O God how hard is my life.') The work of the hero remains unfinished but who will do it if not he?

Kerins' dream team is:

1. Damien Fitzhenry
(Wexford)

2. Willie O'Connor     3. Noel Hickey     4. Ollie Canning
(Kilkenny)          (Kilkenny)         (Galway)

5. Brian Whelehan     6. Ken McGrath     7. Tommy Walsh
(Offaly)           (Waterford)         (Kilkenny)

8. Tony Browne         9. Joe Cooney
(Waterford)          (Galway)

10. Eddie Brennan     11. John Troy     12. Henry Shefflin
(Kilkenny)          (Offaly)          (Kilkenny)

13. Eoin Kelly     14. Dan Shanahan     15. Martin Comerford
(Tipperary)          (Waterford)         (Kilkenny)

*Right:* Primrose and Blue: John Tiernan with some friends from Guatemala in the Roscommon colours in August 2007 on his now annual visit to the country.

*Facing page:* Fair play: John Tiernan (far right) presents the Fair Trade award in Roscommon in 2007. John Maughan (far left) was there to lend his support.

# Walk Tall

A man is only as tall as the sum of his deeds. By that criterion, John Tiernan is the tallest man I know.

As a club footballer Tiernan has been in the right place at the right time. As a county player, though, he has not been so fortunate with his timing. His emergence on the club scene coincided with the arrival of St Brigids' most successful import.

'St Brigids had not won a county final for over twenty-five years. One of the leading lights in the club is Seán Kilbride who had played on the same Mayo team as John O'Mahony. Seán was instrumental in luring John to manage us. He came for the 1997 Championship campaign between managing Leitrim and Galway. For years St Brigids were a "nearly team". Our fortunes were transformed with John's involvement in our set-up and we won the county title under him that year. Although he left us to take the Galway job he still kept in touch and we stayed in the winning habit and John was involved with us again when we went on to take the Connacht title.'

How did O'Mahony benefit the team?

'John has great presence in the dressing room. With his record, you want to listen to every word he has to say. People talk about his great tactical ability but to me the thing that really stands out about him is his man-management skills. He just gives you the most amazing self-belief. He convinces you that you are the best player in your position and you go out there and take on the best.'

As St Brigids' star rose so did Tiernan's and he found himself wearing the primrose and blue of Roscommon. At the time the county team

was in something of disarray on and especially off the field with a series of high profile disciplinary problems culminating in the public relations debacle of the 'nude pool playing' incident, which featured some high profile county players. High profile managers like Tommy Carr and Val Daly were brought in to try and solve the problem and restore order to the camp but the problems did not go away. Tiernan is not going to betray any secrets. 'Things happened which everybody knows about. It would be fair to say that they did not help us to win any games and they created a bit of a media circus. Roscommon football was defined more by what happened off the pitch than what happened on it and that's never the best situation.'

John Maughan was brought in to restore discipline. And restore it he did but results did not improve and Maughan sensationally resigned in the course of the League campaign in 2008, following some humiliating defeats and verbal abuse from a section of the Roscommon fans.

'The fans were unhappy because we were not winning matches. The one thing, though, was that John Maughan worked very hard to try and improve things for Roscommon football and nobody can take that away from him.'

2006 was a great year for Roscommon football after a number of years of decline. The high point was Roscommon's minors victory over favourites Kerry in the All-Ireland minor final. Another noteworthy achievement came when Roscommon club side St Brigids won their first Connacht club title. It was right and fitting that at the Roscommon People of the Year awards that November people from both teams were honoured. The St Brigids player to be singled out was the Roscommon forward, John Tiernan. However, despite his considerable achievements on the pitch, Tiernan's recent fame in Roscommon has as much to do with his off-the-ball activities. It started in February 2006 when he quit his job as a teacher and went to Guatemala, having heard reports of the devastation wreaked by Hurricane Stan. 'I always had a desire to do some work in the Third World. I just always believed we had everything easy over here and we had a huge debt to pay to people less fortunate than us.'

Based in a village called Pacaya beside Santiago, he got immersed in a huge housing project. A landslide killed hundreds and uprooted thousands in that poverty-infested region. From the moment he entered the area, John was confronted by intense need. To see this on television is akin to watching *Desperate Housewives* or *The Simpsons*. 'You say to yourself this can not really happen. But when the stark reality is but feet away from you, it is frightening in the extreme.'

The agonising tyranny of the plight of the majority struck him most forcefully on a visit to the slums, a far cry from the paradisal world of the leafy suburbs that are home to the wealthy elite. There the diet of mystically nourishing pap of half-formed truths that he had been fed about the advances in the lot of the poor retreated into the womb of delusion. Guatemala is a highly stratified, paternalistic society without even a notion of noblesse oblige. It seems that the lot of the poor is to live frugally on the crumbs from the wealthy elite's tables. Extreme poverty sucks the vitality out of a community as a bee sucks honey out of a flower. It is a monument to broken hearts and foiled aspirations, to innumerable tales of sadness and dawning shreds of hope. By day Tiernan built houses, by night he taught English in the local schools. Education was crucial because the whole area was locked into the monstrous barbarism of child labour.

'You could not but be moved by what you saw. I think of getting on a bus to go to work and there would be kids as young as nine and ten there with little machettes going off to cut down trees to make a living. Child labour is horrific to see.'

It sounds like a macabre plot from a novel by Charles Dickens. However, the problem of child exploitation in Guatemala is fact, not fiction. There are unknown thousands of child labourers in the country with poverty being the single most important factor contributing to this human tragedy. Parents with large families hate to send their children to work but the options before them are stark: starve at home or survive at work. On low wages a family cannot survive with just one wage earner. Where child labour is available in the market employers simply substitute them for their adult labour since they can bully them into accepting low wages.

The biggest offenders are the labour intensive industries. Employers like children because they learn the lessons of the job quicker than adults. The problem is not the product of inadequate laws but a failure to implement them. Child exploitation is a long way from the top of the political agenda in Guatemala. There are thousands of victims to this modern day blot on the face of humanity, and every one tells the same story. Hunger. The death of hope. A person, it is held, can become accustomed to anything, but child labour for these people is a recurring nightmare. Here as in most places, money, or more precisely the lack of it, makes all the difference. It is difficult not to succumb to a great sense of the desolation of life that sweeps all around like a tidal wave, drowning all in its blackness. The economic, political and cultural disadvantages suffered by these children are a violation of justice and a serious threat to their lives. For all the talk of children's rights many children have not significantly improved their lot or achieved legal, economic or cultural parity. Exposure to this environment was a watershed for John Tiernan.

'When I came back home, I was a real pain for the first few months. I was questioning everything; why do you need that, why do you need this? But you can't just head off to the mountains and live like a hermit in Ireland. You just have to get back into life here and do what you can for people out there. I only did it for three months, but they have to do it for the rest of their lives.'

John quickly got involved in a number of fund-raising projects like a dinner dance and sports auction. He knew that charity was not enough. His is a philosophy of a hand-up, not a handout. The key was sustainable development. Accordingly, he set up an import export jewellery business, drawing on the work of a group of widowed women in Guatemala who had formed a co-op. When he returned to teaching in Marist College in Athlone, he recruited the services of its transition year and also the transition year students in the Convent of Mercy in Roscommon to help run the business. One of the signs of his success is that his active campaigning work has made Athlone a recognised FairTrade Town and he was part of the Athlone FairTrade Committee on his return from Guatemala. He now spends a lot of his time addressing schools and promoting FairTrade products to try to guard against child labour and worker exploitation. John has recently begun to bring a new dimension to his development work by having the co-operative manufacture biros in the colours of each county in Ireland and retailing them around the country.

'The bottom line is that these people don't need volunteers. They need money. Labour is cheap out there and they can find ten workers out there to do what I did. It's all about awareness because these people have nothing. That's why I've done more work since I came home than I did when I was out there.'

Despite the intensity of his commitment to such a serious cause the most striking thing about spending time in his company is that he laughs a lot. Laughter is in his genes. He is a first cousin of the uncrowned king of Irish comedy, Tommy Tiernan.

His sister, Eleanor, is a gifted comedian and rising star who supported Tommy in his smash Vicar Street show Bovinity in 2007–08, seamlessly weaving GAA jokes into her act. In January 2008 the Sunday Tribune picked her as one of their people to watch in the future.

John has made his own small mark in the world of show business. After St Brigids won the Roscommon county title in 2005, John and another Roscommon star, Karol Mannion, became the West of Ireland's answer to Simon and Garfunkel, with a song to the tune of Christy Moore's 'Jockser goes to Stuttgart'. It became the theme tune to the county final DVD. He nearly chokes with laughter when asked if a career in music or an appearance on Celebrity You're A Star beckons: 'Let's just say Louis Walsh has not been ringing me to offer me a recording contract!'

Tiernan has also started to make his mark in coaching, managing the highly successful St Brigids Under-21 team. John began his dream team with one of the great characters in the game. Shane Curran was in a well-known nightclub when he fell into conversation with a complete stranger. The combination of the loud music and the effects of a few glasses of something stronger than lemonade meant that the communication levels were not as they might have been. As they shook hands before parting Curran received an unusual request: 'Any chance if I give you my address you'd sign one of your CDs and send it on to me?'

A puzzled Curran inquired: 'Who exactly do you think I am?'

'You're the lad from the Saw Doctors, aren't you?'

The team is:

1. Shane Curran
(Roscommon)

| 2. Marc Ó Sé | 3. Cormac MacAnallen | 4. Tom Carr |
|:---:|:---:|:---:|
| (Kerry) | (Tyrone) | (Dublin) |
| 5. Seamus Moynihan | 6. Kieran McGeeney | 7. Seán Óg de Paor |
| (Kerry) | (Armagh) | (Galway) |

8. Dermot Earley          9. Darragh Ó Sé
(Roscommon)                  (Kerry)

| 10. Trevor Giles | 11. Padraig Joyce | 12. Oisín McConville |
|:---:|:---:|:---:|
| (Meath) | (Galway) | (Armagh) |
| 13. Maurice Fitzgerald | 14. Peter Canavan | 15. Colm 'Gooch' Cooper |
| (Kerry) | (Tyrone) | (Kerry) |

## The Last Word

St Francis of Assisi famously said it is in giving that we receive. Both John Tiernan and Alan Kerins do more than alert and alarm anyone willing to listen. Their work strikingly dramatises the poverty of the modern world, perilously ruled by self-interest and economic muscle. Their power is in their capacity to stir our resolve and strengthen the collective will to change. They never doubt that a small group of committed people with ideas and vision can change the world. Why? It is the only thing that ever has. They embody what is best in the west because they live by the motto that giving in its purest form expects nothing in return.

# Epilogue:
## *Too Good to be Forgotten*

What though the radiance which was once so bright
Be now forever taken from my sight,
Though nothing can bring back the hour
Of splendour in the grass, of glory in the flower;
We will grieve not, rather find
Strength in what remains behind.

The lines from William Wordsworth in 'Intimations of Immortality' returned to me with the tragic news of the death of Roscommon footballer Gerard Michael Grogan in a car accident on 10 March 2002.

He first put on the Roscommon jersey with the wonder of a child in front of flickering Christmas lights. Every death is difficult but particularly so when it involves the sudden death of a young person. Yet though we grieve for him, we know that his memory lives on, to speak somehow to people not yet born.

Without him Gaelic football and Connacht are poorer places.

# Index

Page numbers in **bold** indicate photos